BECOMING THE PARENT YOUR TEENAGER NEEDS

Copyright © 2024 by Rodney Gage

Published by Four Rivers Media

All rights reserved. No portion of this book may be reproduced, stored in a retrieval system, or transmitted in any form or by any means—electronic, mechanical, photocopy, recording, scanning, or other—except for brief quotations in critical reviews or articles, without prior written permission of the author.

Unless otherwise stated, all scripture are taken from the Holy Bible, New International Version®, NIV®. Copyright © 1973, 1978, 1984, 2011 by Biblica, Inc.™ Used by permission of Zondervan. All rights reserved worldwide. www.zondervan.com. The "NIV" and "New International Version" are trademarks registered in the United States Patent and Trademark Office by Biblica, Inc.™ Other versions cited are GNB, Good News Bible: The Bible in Today's English Version, ® American Bible Society 1966, 1971, 1976; used by permission, and The Message, the New Testament in Contemporary English, ® 1973 by Eugene H. Peterson, published by NAVPress, Colorado Springs, Colo.; used by permission.

For foreign and subsidiary rights, contact the author.

Cover design by Sara Young
Cover photo by Gabriela Furtado

ISBN: 978-1-959095-17-0   1 2 3 4 5 6 7 8 9 10

Printed in the United States of America

INSPIRATIONS FOR DAILY
ENCOURAGEMENT

BECOMING THE PARENT YOUR TEENAGER NEEDS

RODNEY GAGE

CONTENTS

Acknowledgments ix
Introduction 11
1 SOW IN TEARS . . . REAP WITH JOY! 13
2 YOU MEAN THIS IS NORMAL? 16
3 A REVOLUTIONARY IDEA 19
4 THE FIVE EMOTIONAL GAUGES OF TEENAGERS 22
5 NEEDING GOD 25
6 NEEDING ONE ANOTHER 28
7 AND YOU THOUGHT YOU HAD NEEDS . . . (PART 1) 31
8 AND YOU THOUGHT YOU HAD NEEDS . . . (PART 2) 34
9 THE GAUGE OF BEING NOTICED—ATTENTION 37
10 THE GAUGE OF BEING NOTICED—RESPECT 40
11 THE GAUGE OF BEING NOTICED—VALUED 43
12 THE GAUGE OF BEING NOTICED—APPRECIATION 45
13 THE GAUGE OF ENCOURAGEMENT—NURTURE 48
14 THE GAUGE OF ENCOURAGEMENT—SUPPORT 50
15 THE GAUGE OF EMPATHY—COMFORT 53
16 THE DIRECTION GAUGE—SIGNIFICANCE AND PURPOSE 56
17 THE GAUGE OF SECURITY— PHYSICAL SECURITY 59
18 THE GAUGE OF SECURITY—ACCEPTANCE 62
19 THE GAUGE OF SECURITY—LOVED 65
20 CONGRATULATIONS PARENTS! YOU MAKE A DIFFERENCE 68
21 LOVING UNCONDITIONALLY 71
22 SIX ASSUMPTIONS THAT GET YOU IN TROUBLE 74
23 A PARENT INVESTIGATOR (P.I.) 77
24 HOW EMOTIONAL GAUGES WORK: MEETING NEEDS 80
25 BECOME AN EXPERT GAUGE READER 84
26 THE EIGHT MASKS OF TEENAGERS WITH UNMET NEEDS 87
27 RED ALERT 91
28 SIX WAYS PARENTS SABOTAGE A RELATIONSHIP WITH THEIR TEENAGERS ... 94
29 HOW STRESS AFFECTS NEEDS 98
30 UNMET NEEDS AND FATHERLESS HOMES 102
31 CONNECTIONS 105
32 RELATIONSHIP SKILL #1—CARING 108
33 RELATIONSHIP SKILL #2—TRUSTING 111

34	RELATIONSHIP SKILL #3—GIVING	114
35	RELATIONSHIP SKILL #4—LOVING	117
36	PARENTING STYLES (PART 1)	121
37	PARENTING STYLES (PART 2)	124
38	REVOLUTIONARY RELATIONSHIP BUILDERS	127
39	LOOK IN THE MIRROR AND DISCOVER . . .	130
40	WHEN I WAS A TEENAGER . . .	133
41	MY NEEDS AS A TEENAGER	136
42	MY NEEDS AS AN ADULT	139
43	THE REALITY OF PAST	142
44	THE BEST OF TIMES/THE WORST OF TIMES	145
45	CAUGHT IN PARENT TRAP	149
46	A TIME FOR HEALING	152
47	A TIME FOR FORGIVENESS	155
48	MEETING MY FUTURE NEEDS	158
49	ABC'S FOR THE FUTURE	161
50	DISCOVER, ENERGIZE, FIND, GIVE	164
51	GIVING UNCONDITIONAL LOVE	167
52	REVOLUTIONARY RELATIONSHIP PARENTING	170
53	WHAT TEENAGERS WANT	173
54	WHAT TEENAGERS NEED	176
55	ACTIONS AND ATTITUDES TO MEET: THE NOTICED GAUGE—ATTENTION	179
56	ACTIONS AND ATTITUDES TO MEET: THE NOTICED GAUGE—RESPECT	182
57	ACTIONS AND ATTITUDES TO MEET: THE NOTICED GAUGE—VALUED	185
58	ACTIONS AND ATTITUDES TO MEET: THE NOTICED GAUGE—APPRECIATED	187
59	ACTIONS AND ATTITUDES TO MEET: THE ENCOURAGEMENT GAUGE—NURTURED	190
60	ACTIONS AND ATTITUDES TO MEET: THE ENCOURAGEMENT GAUGE—SUPPORTED	193
61	ACTIONS AND ATTITUDES TO MEET: THE EMPATHY GAUGE—COMFORT	196
62	ACTIONS AND ATTITUDES TO MEET: THE DIRECTION GAUGE—SIGNIFICANCE AND PURPOSE	199
63	ACTIONS AND ATTITUDES TO MEET: THE SECURITY GAUGE—SECURITY	202
64	ACTIONS AND ATTITUDES TO MEET: THE SECURITY GAUGE—ACCEPTANCE	206
65	ACTIONS AND ATTITUDES TO MEET: THE SECURITY GAUGE—LOVED	209
66	ARE YOU WILLING TO CHANGE?	212
67	REVOLUTIONARY INSIGHTS	215
68	OUT-OF-TOUCH PARENTS	218
69	SIX COMMUNICATION BLOCKERS	221
70	ARE YOU LISTENING? TECHNIQUE #1	224

71	ARE YOU LISTENING? TECHNIQUES #2, #3, #4, AND #5	227
72	ARE YOU LISTENING? TECHNIQUES #6, #7, #8, AND #9	230
73	FIVE STEPS TO REDUCING AND RESOLVING CONFLICT	233
74	WHAT TO DO WHEN YOUR TEENAGER WON'T TALK (PART 1)	236
75	WHAT TO DO WHEN YOUR TEENAGER WON'T TALK (PART 2)	239
76	WHEN THEY SAY WHAT THEY NEED, ARE YOU LISTENING?	242
77	IDENTIFY THE WOUNDS: HURT CAUSED BY TEENAGERS	245
78	IDENTIFY THE WOUNDS: HURT CAUSED BY PARENTS	248
79	GRIEF, GUILT, AND OTHER FEELINGS	251
80	FIND REPENTANCE AND FORGIVENESS	254
81	FORGIVE AND BE FREE	257
82	WHEN TO ASK FOR HELP	260
83	WHEN THE HURTING STOPS	263
84	RELATIONSHIP GOALS	265
85	RELATIONSHIP GOAL SETTING	268
86	MAKING YOUR GOALS A REALITY	271
87	HANGING ON TO HOPE	274
88	TOP TEN THINGS PARENTS WOULD LIKE TO HEAR FROM THEIR TEENAGERS	277
89	KEEPING THE RELATIONSHIP REVOLUTION ALIVE	279
90	THE BEST NEWS A PARENT CAN HEAR	282

Endnotes	285
Bibliography	287
Resources	291

ACKNOWLEDGMENTS

I want to thank the incredible team of Four Rivers Media. You are the true heroes behind the scenes to turn my vision for this devotional into a reality.

Thank you to my amazing wife Michelle. You have been my greatest cheerleader and constant support as we have walked side by side for over 30 years. Our children arise and call you "blessed."

And finally, to our daughters Becca and Ashlyn, sons-in-law Daniel and Dillion, and our son Luke. You bring joy to my life in ways that are beyond words. I am proud of each of you for who you have become.

INTRODUCTION

For over 30 years I have interacted with countless parents and teenagers as a pastor and through my travels as an author & speaker. One thing I discovered from the very beginning of my ministry is that parents need all the help, hope, and encouragement they can get as they strive to become the kind of parents their teenagers really need. This is the reason I believe the Lord impressed upon my heart to provide a practical tool for parents that will strengthen their family relationships on a daily basis.

Based on the book *Why Your Kids Do What They Do*, this devotional is designed to be a continuing reference guide to help you effectively meet the key spiritual and emotional needs of your teenager.

From time to time, all parents ask those "why" questions regarding their teen's attitudes and actions. This companion devotional will not only enable you as a parent to understand those "why" questions, but will give you hope, encouragement, and spiritual wisdom as you work through the struggles we all face.

Let the passages of Scripture throughout this devotional be a constant reminder that God loves you and your family very much. More than anything, God wants your family to experience the true benefits and blessings of knowing Him. Even if your teenager doesn't respond to your spiritual guidance, don't give up. Remember God promises, "Never will

I leave you; never will I forsake you" (Heb. 13:5b). God also promises, "His word will not return empty but will accomplish what He desires and achieve the purpose for which He sent it" (Isa. 55:11).

As you read through the various devotions that apply to you as a parent, let the Scripture be a source of healing and comfort concerning the issues of your past or the challenges you're facing right now. It is my prayer that the principles and suggestions outlined in this devotional will allow you to truly experience an unbreakable bond with every member of your family.

I
SOW IN TEARS...REAP WITH JOY!

Gods Speaks...
Psalm 126:5

Recently, some dear friends went through a crisis with their seventeen – year-old daughter Tracy that changed their lives forever. Bob has two beautiful daughters from his first marriage, which ended when the girls were teenagers. Shortly after his divorce, he remarried and had two more daughters. Feeling the responsibility for raising two young children and the demands of his successful career, Bob paid little attention to his older girls.

When the oldest daughter graduated and left for college, Tracy found herself living with her dad, her stepmother, and two baby half-sisters, and feeling strangely unwanted. Tracy immediately latched on to friends for support. With almost no accountability, Tracy spent all her time with her new friends who introduced her to drinking and drugs. These friends offered her the attention and acceptance she craved.

When I noticed Tracy, who was already slender, was losing weight, I asked Bob about it. After several moments of discomfort, Bob finally confessed that Tracy was using drugs. He said, "Rodney, I have done everything I know to do. Nothing works."

Several weeks later, I received a frantic phone call at my office from Bob. "Rodney, can you recommend a good treatment center for Tracy?" He told me Tracy had passed out from a drug overdose. The doctors at the hospital informed Bob that she was addicted to cocaine.

When Tracy returned home from the treatment center, Bob invited me over to talk with them. For the first time, Tracy shared with her father the feelings that led to her rebellious lifestyle of drugs. Feeling that all her parents' attention was devoted to her older sister and two baby stepsisters, as well as the trauma of her parents' divorce, Tracy believed her life didn't matter anymore. She explained that all she wanted was to feel significant. She also expressed a desire for a closer relationship with her mom and dad. Tracy shared how using drugs helped her cope with the pain of rejection. Even though it's been an uphill climb, God is bringing healing and restoration to this family's life.

Psalm 126:5 encourages parents with this promise: "Those who sow in tears will reap with songs of joy."

In between the sowing and the reaping are days of hard work, long hours of great pain, and nearly unbearable moments of incredible tension. Unfortunately, Bob's family shed many tears in their painful, life-changing experience. During this time Bob learned that teenagers who can't find attention, support, acceptance, approval, and affection at home seek other alternatives to get those needs met in their lives. Many times these alternatives are destructive.

My prayer is that through this book you will learn to identify and meet the needs of your teenager and that you might experience fewer days of tears and greater times of joy.

TODAY'S CHALLENGE

Single out one specific behavior in your teenager that has brought the most tears.

TODAY'S REFLECTIONS

- » This study reminds me ...
- » A thought God has brought to mind ...
- » I want to focus on ...

TODAY'S PRAYER

- » Pray for the place in your relationship with your teenager where there are tears. Ask for God's comfort.
- » Pray for the tears your teenager may be weeping inside. Ask God to guide you in helping your teenager turn those tears into joy.

NOTES

_____
_____
_____
_____
_____

2
YOU MEAN THIS IS NORMAL?

God Speaks . . .
Psalm 127:3

I'll never forget one night in my junior year in high school. My friend Dave and I drove home from a Dallas Mavericks basketball game in my dad's brand-new Datsun 280ZX (Google it). Fighting the massive traffic jam after the game, we finally pulled on to the freeway and headed home.

Since it was a school night, our parents told us to come home immediately after the game. Being obedient, responsible young men, Dave and I agreed we could get home faster if I pushed my dad's sports car to the limit. On the freeway I eased up behind a pickup truck traveling about 85 mph. I moved over to pass the pickup at about 100 mph. The guy in the truck pulled up beside us, obviously challenging us to a race. I looked at Dave and said, "I feel the need for speed." We quickly soared to somewhere between 115 to 120 mph. I was a seventeen-year-old kid, and the thought never entered my mind that we might crash or that I was putting our lives in danger. All I wanted to do was leave that pickup truck in my dust. Dave and I celebrated with high fives, as if we had won the Daytona 500. That's when I saw the flashing red lights of not one, but two, police cars in my rearview mirror.

I also failed to consider the consequences of a speeding ticket. The police pulled us over, as well as the guy in the truck. Fortunately, the officer showed great compassion and issued my first speeding ticket for only 105 mph. I must confess, however, my parents were not so compassionate three days later when I mustered up the courage to tell them.

As a parent, have you ever wondered why teenagers do the things they do? Surprisingly, what appears to be risky, bizarre behavior to adults makes perfect sense to teenagers. Yet would a sane, rational adult:

- drive 120 mph on the freeway to show off in front of his friend?
- break up with her boyfriend after dating less than a month to "avoid the pain of breaking up later when it will hurt more"?
- drink from the milk jug, then assure his mother, "It's OK. I'm not sick"?
- look at a room piled high with clean and dirty clothing, books, papers, and empty bags of chips, then ask, "Where's my phone?" (Well, maybe a few adults would do this!)

You get the picture. Every day, growing-up, adolescent behavior appears strange to adults. To teenagers, however, this behavior seems perfectly normal as they assert their independence from their families. Adults shake their heads, wondering what's wrong with teenagers today, and teenagers wonder why adults don't understand them.

The Bible says children are a reward from God. Do you feel like you have been rewarded? If you are having a tough time with your teenager, you may feel as if children, or at least teenagers, are anything but a reward. During these next three months as you work through this devotional book, I pray that you will experience many benefits as you learn how to meet the needs of your teenager in day-to-day living. When that happens, I believe you will see your teenager as a blessed, significant, unique reward from God.

TODAY'S CHALLENGE

Decide if you see your teenager as a reward or a curse and why.

TODAY'S REFLECTIONS

- » This study reminds me …
- » A thought God has brought to mind …
- » I want to focus on …

TODAY'S PRAYER

- » Thank God for this young person He has given you.
- » Pray for God to protect your teenager from the bizarre, but "normal," activities teenagers get into.

NOTES

_____
_____
_____
_____
_____
_____
_____

3
A REVOLUTIONARY IDEA

God Speaks . . .
Luke 15:20-24

Jimmy's curfew was 12:30 on weekends. He faithfully came home at 12:30, turned off the downstairs lights, and climbed the stairs to his room. What his parents didn't know was that shortly after Jimmy came home, he left again through his upstairs bedroom window, slipped across the steep garage roof, climbed down at the far end, and met his buddies up the street. One night Jimmy's dad heard a strange noise coming from Jimmy's room. When he went in to check on his son, he saw the empty bed and the wide-open window. Jimmy's dad shut the window and locked it, then sat downstairs to wait for Jimmy to come home—again.

Why is Jimmy so rebellious? There are many "why" questions parents ask about their teens' behavior. Whether it's normal, although strange, teenage behavior or unhealthy, destructive, inappropriate actions, I believe the answer to all those "why" questions can be summed up in one word—*needs*. Like all of us, teenagers have real, significant, identifiable emotional and relational needs. I believe these basic emotional needs motivate teenagers to do the things they do.

As long as their teenagers are making fairly good grades, and they're not causing problems, most parents think everything is OK. On the other hand, if a teenager creates trouble for the family with a consistent pattern of negative behavior, parents usually take the natural, logical step to correct the problem: ground the teenager for life. I'm not saying there is anything wrong with enforcing consequences for inappropriate behavior. What I am proposing, however, is the revolutionary idea of looking beyond the actions to the motivation. If your teenager fails to respond to your discipline, rather than trying to change the behavior, step back and consider: What are the needs behind my teenager's deeds? What is she trying to tell me through these negative attitudes and actions?

The prodigal son story in Luke 15 is so familiar that we forget the depth of pain behind the story. The father probably asked his own "why" questions.

- What do you think motivated the son to leave his father's house?
- What needs did the father demonstrate to his returning son?
- Think of a time when you felt the same joy exhibited by the father over the homecoming of his son. Write a few thoughts in a journal about your experience. Or, if you are still praying for this type of homecoming, record your feelings while waiting.

TODAY'S CHALLENGE

Look beyond the behavior you identified earlier to see if you can determine a need your teenager feels is missing in his life.

TODAY'S REFLECTIONS

» This study reminds me...
» A thought God has brought to mind...
» I want to focus on...

TODAY'S PRAYER

» Pray for an understanding heart as you live with the day-to-day struggles of your teenager.
» Ask God for the patience and gracious manner of the father in the prodigal son story.

NOTES

4
THE FIVE EMOTIONAL GAUGES OF TEENAGERS

God Speaks . . .
Genesis 28:15

Remember my dad's new 280ZX I mentioned in Day 2? It was beautiful. It was silver and blue, the ultimate car for a Dallas Cowboys' fan, with an awesome stereo and every kind of gadget you could get, including a T-top. The most amazing thing about the car, however, was that it could talk. When it ran low on gas, a female voice would say, "Fuel level is low." If you didn't shut the door completely, the soft voice warned, "Door is open." If you forgot to turn off the lights, she reminded you, "Lights are on." The lady that lived inside that car could tell you anything you wanted to know about that car.

Wouldn't it be great if teenagers came equipped with gauges that indicated when something was wrong? Can you imagine a light that blinks on and off through your teenager's eyes that says, "Affection level is low"; or "Check security need immediately."

Unfortunately, when the emotional needs of teenagers get out of whack, their gauges usually flash warnings through inappropriate, often destructive, behavior. As parents, we must be sensitive to a teenager's basic emotional needs and determine ways to meet those needs. When a teenager's needs are met through healthy relationships with parents and other caring adults, teenagers are more likely to exhibit positive attitudes and positive behavior. When that happens, the emotional gauges that monitor needs quietly return to monitoring the system known as a teenager.

I've taken five basics that I think are critical to a teenager's emotional requirements and formed an easy-to-remember acrostic. The list is not comprehensive, but I believe these basic emotional needs drive your teenager's behavior. Every teenager has a need . . .

to be   Noticed
to receive   Encouragement
to receive   Empathy
to receive   Direction
to receive   Security

The Noticed Gauge—Teenagers need to receive focused attention because they want to be respected as a person, valued for who they are, and appreciated for what they do.

The Encouragement Gauge—Teenagers need to be nurtured as they reach for their dreams and supported when they feel like giving up.

The Empathy Gauge—Teenagers need to receive comfort when they experience pain, sorrow, or despair.

The Direction Gauge—Teenagers need to feel a sense of significance and purpose in their lives.

The Security Gauge—Teenagers need to feel physical security, as well as acceptance, regardless of their flaws and mistakes, and loved no matter what.

You are not alone in trying to figure out how to meet all of these needs. Like the calm, timely voice of the lady who lived in my dad's car comes the powerful assurance that God is with you in this endeavor.

TODAY'S CHALLENGE

Write Genesis 28:15 on a sticky note and place it where you will see it often. Reflect on the depth of God's assurance.

TODAY'S REFLECTIONS

» This study reminds me …
» A thought God has brought to mind …
» I want to focus on …

TODAY'S PRAYER

» Pray that you can hear God's assuring voice as you seek to identify and meet your teenager's needs.
» Ask God for the one ingredient—strength, courage, confidence, peace, joy, assurance—that you need in parenting your teenager.

NOTES

_____
_____
_____
_____
_____

5
NEEDING GOD

God Speaks . . .

2 Corinthians 1:3-4a

Philippians 4:19

God created us with needs. The Creator of the universe could have formed us never to need air or nourishment. He could have given us bodies that never needed sleep or never felt pain. But God created people with needs. Physically we need air, food, water, rest, and protection from the elements. Emotionally God created us to desire acceptance, encouragement, appreciation, and love. A part of these emotional needs involves relationships. A final area of need also includes a need to fill a spiritual void. That void longs for a relationship with a higher being, freedom from guilt, a willingness to forgive and to be forgiven, and a yearning for peace.

Why did God create us with needs? Philippians 4:19 puts it this way:

My God will meet all your needs according to his glorious riches in Christ Jesus.

God created us to need so we will turn to Him on a regular basis. God is our first source for finding comfort in grief, peace in the middle of stress, relationship in loneliness. Whether we are willing to admit it or not, we are needy people. We are people whose emotional pain can only be healed with the spiritual relationship offered by God. People try to handle their emotional pain with drugs, alcohol, numerous relationships, false religions, work, money—none of these work. Ignoring our need for God is also a fruitless venture. The bottom line is: We need God.

Second Corinthians 1:3-4a expresses that God cares about our needs. Does God feel emotions like we do? Many times in the Old Testament, prophets expressed the pain God felt over Israel's sins. Numerous psalms tell of God's emotions. But we see the reality of God's concern when we look at Jesus. Jesus put a face on God. In His face we see weariness, pain, frustration, sadness, compassion, joy. Jesus only performed around thirty miracles in His three years of ministry. Yet, He taught frequently about relationships—the importance of relationships ("Love one another as I have loved you") with startling insights ("Love your enemy"; "Turn the other cheek"; being the "neighbor" in the good Samaritan parable; "Forgive seventy times seven"). God the Father cares for us dearly. Like an earthly parent, He hurts when we hurt and rejoices when we rejoice.

Think about what needs you have and how God meets those needs.

Today I need God to ...

In the past I know God has met my needs by ...

In order for me to help my teenager, I need God to ...

TODAY'S CHALLENGE

Today, notice the needs of those around you. Observe how God meets those needs.

TODAY'S REFLECTIONS

- » This study reminds me ...
- » A thought God has brought to mind ...
- » I want to focus on ...

TODAY'S PAYER

» Thank God for creating you with needs so you will remember to seek Him frequently.
» Ask God to comfort you in the greatest need you have today.

NOTES

6
NEEDING ONE ANOTHER

God Speaks . . .
Genesis 2:15, 18, 21-22
2 Corinthians 1:3-4

God not only created us to need Him, but also to need others. Genesis 2:15 tells us that God and Adam interacted in the garden of Eden. God filled Adam's need for spiritual companionship. Yet God noticed Adam's loneliness (Gen. 2:18). So, He met Adam's need for human relationship and created a companion, Eve (Gen. 2:21-22). God created us to need one another. Yesterday you saw how God created us to need Him for comfort. But look again at 2 Corinthians 1:3-4. The process of needing expands.

The God of all comfort, who comforts us in all our troubles, so that we can comfort those in any trouble with the comfort we ourselves have received from God.

God comforts us so we can comfort others. Through our needs, we relate to one another. We learn how to meet others' needs because we experience God meeting our needs. God comforts us; we in turn can comfort others. As God graciously meets our needs, He wants us to unselfishly meet the needs of others. Children look to parents to meet their needs. Adults look to other adults.

Have you ever had a need met by another person? For example, were you totally dependent on a family member or a friend after an automobile accident or surgery? When your need was the greatest, didn't you appreciate that person more for what they did and said? Once your need was met, you were more willing to meet another's need, knowing how vital that can be.

Some people feel that it is a weakness to need others. True humility recognizes that we can't do everything ourselves. We must depend on others.

- Think of a time when someone met your need. How did you feel about the situation? What was the outcome of the event?
- Think of a time when you were able to meet someone else's need. How did you feel about helping that person?
- How can understanding that we need one another help you in parenting your teenager?

TODAY'S CHALLENGE

Think of someone who has met a need of yours in the recent past. Drop that person a brief note, send a text, or make a telephone call expressing your appreciation for that person's time and energy in caring for you.

TODAY'S REFLECTIONS

» This study reminds me …
» A thought God has brought to mind …
» I want to focus on …

TODAY'S PRAYER

- » Pray for the person who most recently has met a need in your life.
- » Pray that you will be more open to letting others help you as you seek to meet the needs of your teenager.

NOTES

7
AND YOU THOUGHT YOU HAD NEEDS... (PART I)

God Speaks...
Luke 2:52

We know almost nothing of Jesus' teenage years. Don't you wish we knew how Joseph and Mary felt watching those gangly arms and legs take on muscle and seeing the awkward stride of His early teenage years turn into a somber stride? Don't you wonder if Jesus had the normal moods swings of a developing teenager and how His moods affected the whole household? Could Jesus express His needs better than today's teenager? Did the extra confusion of a changing body contribute to His sense of need?

We all have physical, emotional, and spiritual needs. However, mix in the everyday growing-up, developmental needs of teenagers and suddenly teenagers are overwhelmed with neediness. Here are three key areas of normal teenager development.

Physical growth creates awkward, uncoordinated, embarrassed, confused teenagers. It probably seems like yesterday that those new jeans fit your son; today those same jeans don't reach to his socks. Tennis shoes no longer wear out; they "grow out." Physical development can he spasmodic, quick, uneven, and often painful. Heart and lung capacity double as stomachs increase almost one-third in size. (You already knew this because you've watched the grocery bills climb!) Pimples are a teenager's worst nightmare. Whatever part of the body makes the teenager the most uncomfortable is the part the teenager tries to cover up or tugs at or constantly complains about. During this time, parents must be careful not to confuse attitude and growth. Rapidly growing teenagers are like small babies who also grow quickly—both need a lot of sleep! Don't confuse your teenager's need for sleep, or the companion feeling of being wiped out, with laziness, especially if your teenager has grown several inches over the last three to six months.

Sexual growth stirs deep feelings from guilt to amazement. Teenagers are one, big, walking hormone. Guys think about sex; girls think about love. Hair crops up in strange places. Swelling buds become breasts and hips fill out in girls. Guys face new experiences like wet dreams and a surprisingly squeaky voice. (Have you ever noticed how thirteen – to fifteen-year-old guys rarely answer the phone?) Sexual changes prepare a teenager for sexual experiences, but teenagers lack the maturity to accept the responsibility associated with sexual intercourse. Hormones not only relate to sexual development, but also influence ricocheting emotions and bizarre behavior.

Emotional growth puts a teenager (and parents) on a huge emotional roller coaster of exaggerated feelings. A simple "Good morning!" can bring a flood of tears or a tongue-lashing. The greatest joy can be followed quickly by anger. Parents operate from a disadvantage unless they assume that everything in the life of the teenager is a crisis. To a teenager it usually is.

TODAY'S CHALLENGE

Notice where your teenager is in the developmental process that involves physical, sexual, and emotional growth. How has your teenager responded to these rapid changes?

TODAY'S REFLECTIONS

- » This study reminds me ...
- » A thought God has brought to mind ...
- » I want to focus on ...

TODAY'S PRAYER

- » Thank God for the miracle of growth.
- » Pray for the patience to survive your teenager's miracle.

NOTES

_____
_____
_____
_____
_____
_____
_____

8
AND YOU THOUGHT YOU HAD NEEDS... (PART 2)

God Speaks...
Luke 2:52

Do you think Jesus was instantly wise, or did He struggle with concrete and abstract concepts? Don't you wonder if Jesus had difficulty communicating with His mom and dad?

Social, mental, and spiritual needs contribute to a teenager's developmental growth. Many changes take place in your teenager during these years. Once children begin to look like adults, some parents forget that these young people still struggle with many developmental issues. Knowing what's going on in the different areas of their development will help you determine what emotional needs they require.

In *social development* the teenager moves from a same-sex, best friend relationship of younger youth to a circle of friends where the teenager interacts with both sexes. Teenagers try on different personalities to see which feels comfortable and how others respond. "Today I'm going to get along with everybody," Callie announced one morning. That personality change lasted until her younger brother spilled his milk into her hook bag. Teenagers worry about what others say about them, how others see them, what others think about them.

Mental growth doesn't necessarily involve the amount of information a teenager is learning, but the way that information is processed. Younger teenagers are concrete thinkers, seeing life in basic terms—right or wrong, black or white, true or false. Around the eighth grade, teenagers begin to process thoughts abstractly. Other people's beliefs and opinions expand their thoughts and challenge their thinking. In the transition from concrete thoughts to abstract thoughts, teenagers face doubt and indecision. Many parents panic during a teenager's early mental development when their child who brought home good grades suddenly becomes academically challenged. Add to the mix a teenager's rapidly growing body, new sexual stirrings, shifting relationships, the desire for independence, the fear of the unknown—all these areas cause stress that stretches a teenager to the point where school becomes a low priority. Rather than attacking your teenager for poor grades, determine the number of changes occurring in your teenager's life to see how these might be influencing school performance.

Spiritual growth can be a roller coaster of highs and lows. Teenagers who experience their faith through their parents must struggle to find a faith of their own. Doubts can be very real during this time in their lives. Some youth feel they let God down with their doubts; others use their doubts as an excuse to bail out of religion. Youth exposed to biblical absolutes through home and church might question those beliefs and values when exposed to secular humanism and moral relativism. Social relationships affect how they feel about themselves and how they perceive God feels about them. Throughout their seeking runs their quest for values and standards that fit the person they want to become.

TODAY'S CHALLENGE

Notice where your teenager is in the developmental process that involves their social, mental, and spiritual growth. How is your teenager responding to these changes?

TODAY'S REFLECTIONS

- » This study reminds me ...
- » A thought God has brought to mind ...
- » I want to focus on ...

TODAY'S PRAYER

- » Pray especially for your teenager's salvation if he or she has not accepted Jesus as his or her personal Savior.

NOTES

_____
_____
_____
_____
_____
_____

9
THE GAUGE OF BEING NOTICED—ATTENTION

God Speaks...
Proverbs 27:23

Sheep need a shepherd for one very important reason: They tend to nibble themselves lost. To a hungry sheep the grass looks just a little more tasty over there. Soon the greedy sheep has eaten himself away from the herd and put himself in danger. The attentive shepherd knows which sheep have a tendency to venture off by themselves. He knows to pay attention so he can keep his sheep safe and •unharmed.

Parents are the shepherds of their families. Without close attention, an inquisitive, curious teenager can nibble himself lost. Here's what is involved in the *attention* need under the gauge of being noticed.

Teenagers need to receive focused attention because they want to be respected as people, valued for who they are, and appreciated for what they do.

Too often we barely focus on the person standing in front of us, much less on a teenager hiding in her room or one whose busy schedule keeps him out of the house. How do teenagers get attention? Hair and clothing choices may be one way. Picking on a younger sibling may be another. How about their loud music? Doesn't that say, "I'm home! Just wanted you to notice!" Angry words, slamming doors, even the dreaded silent treatment all scream for attention. Unfortunately, the attention these actions draw can be more negative than positive. Teenagers who lack parental attention in positive ways will settle for negative strokes, rather than feel no strokes at all.

Focused attention begins with the basics of communication—turn off the TV; put down the phone, make eye contact; listen, don't talk; repeat feelings you hear expressed. Focused attention validates the life of your teenager by saying, "You are worth my time, my effort, my energy."

- Describe the last time you gave your teenager your undivided attention.
- How did you feel about the experience?
- How do you think your teenager felt about the experience?
- In what other ways do you pay attention to your teenager?
- On a scale of 1 (low) to 10 (high), how would your teenager gauge the need for attention?

TODAY'S CHALLENGE

Watch how others demand your attention, including your teenager. How do you respond to each person's demand, especially to your teenager's request for attention?

TODAY'S REFLECTIONS

» This study reminds me …
» A thought God has brought to mind …
» I want to focus on …

TODAY'S PRAYER

- » Thank God for giving attention to your life.
- » Pray that you will see with new eyes when your teenager requests your attention.

NOTES

10
THE GAUGE OF BEING NOTICED—RESPECT

God Speaks . . .
James 2:3-8

1 Peter 2:17

Peter began his letter with the basic element of treating other people as human beings with personal dignity. Sadly, we often fail to respect those closest to us, assuming they'll understand our moods and take whatever emotional garbage we dump on them.

James pleads for respect with an example that relates well to teenagers, whose clothing, hairstyles, and body decorations can create barriers with parents. On the other hand, if parents are willing to look past the superficial, they will find teenagers worth respecting.

Teenagers need to receive focused attention because they want to be *respected* as people, valued for who they are, and appreciated for what they do.

Disrespecting others, what teenagers call "dissing," is a popular behavior among young people. They learn this disrespectful attitude by copying "the bad boy" personalities on video games, television or mimicking their disrespectful peers at school. Even though our kids may laugh at the caustic comments and crude actions from others on TV, as parents we can't lower ourselves to that behavior. If we want our teenagers to be respectful, we must model respect in the home.

Do you respect the privacy and possessions of your teenager? Do you knock before entering a room with a closed door? Do you respect what is in your teenager's room—a diary or journal, notes and letters, pictures, magazines? Unless you can link a dramatic change in behavior with a pattern of disobedience or some other warning action, you need to respect your teenager's things.

Do you ask before borrowing clothing? (OK, I know teenagers frequently "borrow" clothing from you, but remember, you are the adult. Model the ideal, the better way.)

Do you respect your teenager's ideas and opinions? Do you ask your teenager for input into activities that involve them? Do you listen to what they say, even when today's opinion changes tomorrow? (Remember, they are trying on different personalities to discover who they are. They try on different philosophies too.)

Do you respect your teenager's personhood? Do you avoid put–downs, name-calling, all teasing that belittles the teenager? Are you careful about when you discipline your teenager? For example, do you talk to your teenager in private, rather than in front of her friends?

- Describe a time when respect was a problem between you and your teenager.
- How did you feel about the experience?
- How do you think your teenager felt about the experience?
- Were you able to resolve the issue? How?
- In what ways do you show respect to your teenager?
- On a scale of 1 (low) to 10 (high), how would your teenager gauge the need for respect?

TODAY'S CHALLENGE

List areas where you want others' respect. Place a check mark by the areas where you respect your teenager. How do the two areas compare?

TODAY'S REFLECTIONS

- » This study reminds me ...
- » A thought God has brought to mind ...
- » I want to focus on ...

TODAY'S PRAYER

- » Pray that God will show you the importance of respect today.
- » Thank God for respecting you by giving us freedom of choice.

NOTES

_____
_____
_____
_____
_____
_____
_____

11
THE GAUGE OF BEING NOTICED—VALUED

God Speaks...
Philippians 4:8

Paul knew the importance of character being of the highest standard. Truth, nobleness or respect, knowing right from wrong, desiring purity, a reputation worth admiring, excellence in morality, being worthy of others' praise—these make up a person's ideal character. Eugene Peterson expresses this verse in his unique translation called *The Message:* "I'd say you'll do best by filling your minds and meditating on things true, noble, reputable, authentic, compelling, gracious—the best, not the worst; the beautiful, not the ugly; things to praise, not things to curse."

Paul urged Christians to "think on these things," to hold on to these higher standards in life. Parents need to remember this verse as they model behavior and attitudes for their teenagers. Parents often get so focused on the negatives in their teenager's life that they forget to look for the best. Look for these good qualities in your teenager, then praise the best you find.

Teenagers need to receive focused attention because they want to be respected as people, *valued* for who they are, and appreciated for what they do.

Since teenagers are in the process of becoming, issues of character, values, standards, and personal qualities are forming. Yet even while your teenager tests and accepts or rejects these issues, your teen wants to feel that he or she is someone special. That specialness doesn't come from outward beauty, but from internal qualities—someone whose character can be admired. You value your teenager because you have been valued by God and because your teenager was created by God.

- Describe the last time you showed your teenager you valued him or her.
- How did you feel about the experience?
- How do you think your teenager felt about the experience?
- In what other ways do you value your teenager?
- On a scale of 1 (low) to 10 (high), how would your teenager gauge the need to be valued?

TODAY'S CHALLENGE

Make a list of the positive values and characteristics you see in your teenager. Focus on that list today.

TODAY'S REFLECTIONS

» This study reminds me …
» A thought God has brought to mind …
» I want to focus on …

TODAY'S PRAYER

» Select one of the areas mentioned in Philippians 4:8 and ask God to show you how you can develop a stronger character in that area.
» Pray that God will show you more areas in your teenager's life that have positive qualities.

12
THE GAUGE OF BEING NOTICED—APPRECIATION

God Speaks . . .
Matthew 25:21
1 Thessalonians 5:13

Jesus told a parable of the master who left funds in his servants' care. As a result of their wise investments, two of the three servants heard the statement every person wants to hear after successfully completing a task—"Well done!" Paul also recognized the value of praising others for their work. Everyone wants to be appreciated for the work that is completed, even the most menial task.

Teenagers need to receive focused attention because they want to be respected as people, valued for who they are, and *appreciated* for what they do.

Value shows attention to a teenager because of the teenager's character and standards. Appreciation expresses attention to a teenager because of the teen's performance. The enemy of appreciation is being taken for granted. Teenagers feel ignored and overlooked when no one recognizes when a job is completed, especially if the task took effort. They want to be appreciated for their accomplishments. When a person is recognized for an accomplishment and praised for that work, they are more likely to repeat the positive behavior. Unfortunately, parents expect certain behavior and forget to thank their teenager or acknowledge the work when a task is completed, even if it's done well.

Appreciation starts with recognizing that a task has been completed. This includes regular chores, as well as special activities. Express appreciation for the completion of a task or for your teenager's positive attitude toward the task. Verbal appreciation can be shared both privately with your teenager and publicly to others. Try to catch your teenager doing something right, then applaud your teenager verbally and often. I believe that five very important words parents can say to their teenager are "You did a great job."

- Describe the last time you told your teenager you appreciated him or her for doing a job well.
- How did you feel about the experience?
- How do you think your teenager felt about the experience?
- In what other ways do you show appreciation to your teenager?
- On a scale of 1 (low) to 10 (high), how would your teenager gauge the need to be appreciated?

TODAY'S CHALLENGE

Make a list of chores you expect your teenager to complete. These can be regular chores, such as taking out the garbage, or occasional tasks, such as mowing the lawn or babysitting. Mark each task that you regularly thank your teenager for doing. What task is your teenager working on today? How can you share your appreciation for completing that task?

TODAY'S REFLECTIONS

- » This study reminds me ...
- » A thought God has brought to mind ...
- » I want to focus on ...

TODAY'S PRAYER

- » Pray for the many tasks your teenager must do today. Some are so mundane that they become boring; others are so difficult that they create anxiety.
- » Pray that you will adopt a more appreciative spirit toward all family members for what they do for the family.

NOTES

_____
_____
_____
_____
_____
_____
_____
_____
_____

13
THE GAUGE OF ENCOURAGEMENT— NURTURE

God Speaks...
Romans 15:5
Hebrews 10:24
1 Thessalonians 5:11

Just as God encourages us through Jesus Christ, parents can be cheerleaders, urging their teenagers to reach for the dreams they have. The writer of Hebrews saw the need of encouraging others to love and to healthy actions. Paul, in Thessalonians, saw the value of mutual nurturing.

Teenagers need to be *nurtured* as they reach for their dreams and supported when they feel like giving up.

Nurturing is the active part of encouragement. It cultivates, nourishes, and develops the dreams, hopes, and goals of your teenager. For many younger teenagers their future dreams may only be about what's happening this weekend. Most older teens, however, dream about life beyond high school.

Nurturing includes helping your teenager define and set a goal. Dreaming is the easy part; making the dream happen takes encouragement, whether it's financial support, exposure to different resources, vocational counseling, job opportunities, or a variety of experiences.

The Gauge of Encouragement—Nurture **49**

Occasionally, a teenager struggles to define a dream. You can offer help by encouraging your teenager to build off of the gifts and abilities you see in your teenager. Point out ways people today make a difference. Expose him to people with different hobbies or professions who might spark a dream in your teenager's imagination.

- Describe the last time you nurtured your teenager's dream.
- How did you feel about the experience?
- How do you think your teenager felt about the experience?
- In what other ways do you nurture or encourage your teenager?
- On a scale of 1 (low) to 10 (high), how would your teenager gauge the need to be nurtured or encouraged?

TODAY'S CHALLENGE

Listen for a dream you hear your teenager express. What will it take to make that dream a reality?

TODAY'S REFLECTIONS

» This study reminds me …
» A thought God has brought to mind …
» I want to focus on …

TODAY'S PRAYER

» Pray for your teenager's dreams and desires. Ask God to show you how those dreams can come true.
» Thank God for the times when you have lived your dream. Ask God for forgiveness if you are still bitter about a dream that did not happen.

14
THE GAUGE OF ENCOURAGEMENT — SUPPORT

God Speaks...
Matthew 11:28

Galatians 6:2

"Come to me... and I will give you rest," Jesus promised. How calming these words are to the person caught in today's stress. The level of stress teenagers experience today amazes researchers. They even have a new name for the high stress caused by technology—"techno-stress." The word pictures of these two verses is similar. Each offers the idea of someone walking beside another in a time of stress, discouragement, disappointment, or anxiety. Everyone needs someone who will share the load.

Teenagers need to be nurtured as they reach for their dreams and *supported* when they feel like giving up.

I played a lot of tennis when I was growing up, even in high school and college. Even though my dad traveled most of the time, I often would look up in the stands and see him join my mother late in a match. His determination to be there gave me the boost I needed to finish the match, even though minutes before I had been physically exhausted.

Support can include verbal or written encouragement. Two modern "inventions" that enhance support are sticky notes and the smart phone.

Stick notes of encouragement in your teenager's school books, on the bathroom mirror, on a favorite piece of sports equipment, in a shoe. Send your teenager text messages, voice memos of encouragement and support.

Times when teenagers need support might be the night before a big test, the day they take SATs or other standardized testing that determines their future, when they try out for the team, anytime your teenager participates in a special event. Offer support when times get rough and they don't think they'll finish the project. Encourage them as they're getting over a bumpy relationship, or anytime they get discouraged for whatever reason.

- Describe the last time you showed your support for your teenager.
- How did you feel about the experience?
- How do you think your teenager felt about the experience?
- In what other ways do you support your teenager?
- On a scale of 1 (low) to 10 (high), how would your teenager gauge the need to feel supported?

TODAY'S CHALLENGE

Look for a way to support your teenager today—either through your attendance at an important function, through a written note, by an encouraging pat on the back, or a few words of praise.

TODAY'S REFLECTIONS

» This study reminds me ...
» A thought God has brought to mind ...
» I want to focus on ...

TODAY'S PRAYER

- » Pray about an area in your life where you are discouraged. Ask God to help you with this discouragement.
- » Pray for an area of your teenager's life in which the teenager is discouraged. Ask God to show you how you can help in that disappointment.

NOTES

15
THE GAUGE OF EMPATHY–COMFORT

God Speaks . . .
Psalm 23:4

2 Corinthians 2:7

The Bible contains numerous expressions of comfort. God gives the greatest comfort, as expressed in Psalm 23. Even if you're not a shepherd, you know the value of one who knows the way and protects you along that way. The shepherd's rod kept the sheep headed in the right direction. The shepherd's staff pulled sheep back to safety when they wandered too far or fell in a crevice.

Because God comforts us, we can comfort others. The comfort Paul suggested in 2 Corinthians concerned a person opposed to Paul's message and leadership. Paul wrote the letter directing the church family to forgive and comfort the person involved. Parents can offer even greater comfort to their families.

Teenagers need to receive *comfort* when they experience pain, sorrow, or despair.

Comfort is one of the greatest needs teenagers have, yet few can articulate this need. Rarely does a teenager walk into the house and announce, "I've had a bad day. Will someone please comfort me?" However, your teenager may slam through the house or sulk to the bedroom.

The slumped shoulders and downcast eyes tip off their discouragement or despair. Much of the time teenagers hurt emotionally. Parents yell at them. A buddy moves away. A friend breaks a trust. The "in" group rejects them. School authorities demand academic excellence. A broken relationship can create the same traumatic grief for a teenager as a physical death. Unfortunately, death is very real to teenagers who see their classmates harmed on and off school campuses; who have friends killed in automobile accidents, many involving alcohol; who lose cherished grandparents, even parents.

Teenagers do not always make it easy for parents to comfort them. Embarrassed by their emotions, some teenagers prefer to hide the hurt. Others hold back their feelings, anticipating a parental lecture instead of comfort. A few teenagers, struggling with rapidly developing bodies, don't feel comfortable being hugged or touched, even by a parent. Learning how to comfort your teenager is almost by trial and error.

- Describe the last time you comforted your teenager.
- How did you feel about the experience?
- How do you think your teenager felt about the experience?
- In what other ways do you comfort your teenager?
- On a scale of 1 (low) to 10 (high), how would your teenager gauge the need to be comforted?

TODAY'S CHALLENGE

Pray for comfort today for your teenager. Every time you think about it, lift up your teenager in prayer.

TODAY'S REFLECTIONS

» This study reminds me ...
» A thought God has brought to mind ...
» I want to focus on ...

TODAY'S PRAYER

» Thank God for the many times you've felt His comfort toward you.
» Pray for the sensitivity to offer comfort in an acceptable way for your teenager.

NOTES

_____
_____
_____
_____
_____
_____
_____
_____
_____
_____
_____
_____

16
THE DIRECTION GAUGE— SIGNIFICANCE AND PURPOSE

God Speaks . . .
Proverbs 20:5
John 10:10b

The "man of understanding" in Proverbs discovered his purpose in life and assessed its value. Parents aid teenagers in discovering and assessing the purposes in their teenagers' lives. This is an excellent opportunity for parents to offer assurance, guidance, hope, and help. Then, both parent and teenager can experience the abundant, full life promised by God through faith in Jesus Christ.

Teenagers need to feel a sense of *significance and purpose* in their lives.

The number one question teenagers ask during their developmental years is "Who am I?"—Who am I physically, sexually, emotionally, in my relationships, in my faith, in my values? Teens want assurance that their presence on earth is important and valuable to someone. They don't want to feel like a big zero, like someone's "mistake." In the same way that teenagers try on different personalities to see which one fits the best, they also try on different projects to see which helps them feel significant. Some adults see this shifting from project to project as a lack of commitment, but usually teenagers are just trying to figure out what works for them. If teenagers don't see themselves as significant in a positive way, they may look for ways to be significant in a negative, more risky fashion.

Many teenagers believe they can make a difference in the world today. They are determined to learn from their parents' mistakes and to make the future better. These teenagers can serve in the community, through the church, at their schools. Activities like mission trips and service projects teach the teenager the value of life and the importance of making a difference. Families who work together with their teenagers on service projects model for their teenagers how to achieve significance and purpose.

- Describe the last time you helped your teenager feel a sense of significance and purpose.
- How did you feel about the experience?
- How do you think your teenager felt about the experience?
- In what other ways do you help your teenager feel a sense of significance and purpose?
- On a scale of 1 (low) to 10 (high), how would your teenager gauge the need to feel a sense of significance and purpose?

TODAY'S CHALLENGE

Does your teenager see you serving others? How? When?

TODAY'S REFLECTIONS

» This study reminds me...
» A thought God has brought to mind...
» I want to focus on...

TODAY'S PRAYER

» Pray that the behavior and attitude you model for your teenager includes how you value others as significant.

NOTES

17
THE GAUGE OF SECURITY — PHYSICAL SECURITY

God Speaks...
Deuteronomy 31:6
Proverbs 14:26

The comforting words of Deuteronomy assure us of God's eternal presence. Because God meets our needs for security, we can face life with confidence and strength and pass on the same assurance and strength to our teenagers. The writer of Proverbs also realized the need for home to be a haven of safety.

Teenagers need to feel *physical security*, as well as acceptance, regardless of their flaws and mistakes, and loved no matter what.

Security has several sides to it—protection, safety, stability, boundaries that allow freedom and protect from harm. Teenagers desire a stable environment. An unstable environment may be caused by dysfunctional parents, job changes, shifting economics, a move to another place, the addition of grandparents to the household, or the serious illness of a family member. When Sarah's parents divorced shortly after she turned thirteen, Casey, Sarah's closest friend, feared her own parents would divorce, too, although her parents' marriage was strong. Casey needed regular assurance that her family would remain intact.

In addition to offering a safe environment, most teenagers want some kind of boundaries that give them specific limits in their actions, while allowing them some freedom and independence. As they get older, they need help in defining and setting personal boundaries in their own lives.

Peer Pressure to conform and go along with what everyone else thinks, says and does is what gets many teens in trouble. Equip your teens to ask themselves the following questions will help them set personal boundaries. For example; when am I most tempted? Where am I most tempted? With whom am I most tempted? What will be my decision before I'm tempted? Knowing the answers to these questions in advance will help your teenager be proactive and give them the security and courage they need to avoid temptation and stay true to the boundaries they set for themselves.

- Describe the last time your teenager felt secure because of something you did or said.
- How did you feel about the experience?
- How do you think your teenager felt about the experience?
- In what other ways do you help your teenager feel secure?
- On a scale of 1 (low) to 10 (high), how would your teenager gauge the need to feel secure?

TODAY'S CHALLENGE

Walk through your home, noting the effort you've taken to make your home secure. Every time you see a safety device, consider what kind of mental and emotional security you offer your teenager.

TODAY'S REFLECTIONS

» This study reminds me …
» A thought God has brought to mind …
» I want to focus on …

TODAY'S PRAYER

» Pray for God's safety net to keep your teenager from danger.

NOTES

_____
_____
_____
_____
_____
_____
_____
_____
_____
_____
_____
_____
_____

18
THE GAUGE OF SECURITY—ACCEPTANCE

God Speaks . . .
Romans 15:7

In his letter to the Romans, Paul urged the acceptance of Gentiles into the Christian faith. To the Jewish Christians, however, this was like welcoming aliens. Parents are trying to accept and understand aliens, too, except these are called *teenagers*. The point is obvious. God loved "all the world." Acceptance begins with God's acceptance of us; then we accept one another.

Teenagers need to feel physical security, as well as *acceptance*, regardless of their flaws and, mistakes, and feel loved no matter what.

Aren't you thankful God loves us "warts and all." Teenagers want that same kind of acceptance, no matter what flaws they see in their own lives. Parents can he open and accepting by focusing on the best, rather than the worst, they see in their teenagers. That's doesn't mean you ignore inappropriate behavior or faults that need correcting, but you can accept your teenager as God's creation without approving of your teenager's behavior.

Teenagers can be extra-sensitive about how parents feel towards them. Body language, tone of voice, even simple remarks let our young people know whether we accept or reject them. Many times intelligent, wholesome teenagers tell me, "Mom likes my sister more," or "My dad thinks

I'm a geek just because I don't want to play football like my brother." The parents of these teenagers defensively complain, "I love all my children equally." Of course, parents believe they can love their children equally. But in reality, we respond differently to each child. Our ability to spend time with them varies based on the economics of the home at the time they come along. It is difficult to treat our children equally. We would do a lot better if we would treat our children individually, responding to their personalities, abilities, and desires. Be careful not to compare children. Comparison is the enemy of acceptance.

- Describe the last time you showed your teenager acceptance.
- How did you feel about the experience?
- How do you think your teenager felt about the experience?
- In what other ways do you accept your teenager?
- On a scale of 1 (low) to 10 (high), how would your teenager gauge the need to be accepted?

TODAY'S CHALLENGE

Note your body language, eye contact, even your attitude today as you interact with your teenager. What signals do you send unintentionally that may indicate a lack of acceptance? How can you change this?

TODAY'S REFLECTIONS

» This study reminds me ...
» A thought God has brought to mind ...
» I want to focus on ...

TODAY'S PRAYER

» Thank God for accepting you before you were willing to accept Him.
» Pray for God to open your heart and make you more accepting of your teenager "warts and all.

NOTES

___
___
___
___
___
___
___
___
___
___
___
___
___
___
___
___
___
___

19
THE GAUGE OF SECURITY—LOVED

God Speaks . . .
1 Thessalonians 2:8
1 Peter 4:8
1 John 4:11

Examples of God's unconditional love fill the Bible, including His great love for us by sending His Son. With God's amazing love, we can love others. No other place in the teenager's life, except the church, offers the satisfying love, given and expressed unconditionally, that the home does.

Teenagers need to feel physical security, as well as acceptance, regardless of their flaws and mistakes, and *loved* no matter what.

Love is the most basic of needs. That need to feel loved begins at birth and continues to the grave. Love is the foundation for relationships. It encourages, offers empathy, gives attention, and comforts.

Parents offer their teenagers no greater security than the security found in loving unconditionally. This love happens because of a conscious decision to love, not based on feelings. It grows out of a desire to accept a person despite that person's actions or attitudes. Unfortunately, some teenagers feel pressured to earn their parents' love.

A young lady approached me after I spoke in Tampa, Florida. She said, "Rodney, I have been an average student most of my life. I've always felt pressure from my dad to make perfect grades like he did. Last semester I went to a tutor before and after school to help me pull up my grades. I even did extra credit when I didn't really have to. Recently, I brought home the best report card I've ever received—all As and one B." The girl continued, a little more agitated: "I couldn't wait to show my dad, thinking he would be so proud. When I showed him my report card, all he said was, 'That's great, honey, but we need to do something about this B.'"

You can imagine how her father's remarks devastated her. It's OK to expect the best from your teenagers, but be careful that your expectations don't include a demand for perfection.

Unconditional love can be demonstrated with a variety of affection. Teenagers don't make it easy to show them outward affection. Hugs may seem childish, do it anyway. A pat on the back, a high-five or fist pump often say more than words. We've become so frightened in this day of abuse and inappropriate touch that we forget the value of the genuine physical touch. Not only does our heartfelt touch allow you to express your physical affection to your spouse or children, but it also provides an ideal time for meaningful conversation.

- Describe the last time you showed your teenager unconditional love.
- How did you feel about the experience?
- How do you think your teenager felt about the experience?
- In what other ways do you show unconditional love to your teenager?
- On a scale of 1 (low) to 10 (high), how would your teenager gauge the need to be loved unconditionally?

TODAY'S CHALLENGE

Look around you today to evaluate who loves you unconditionally.

TODAY'S REFLECTIONS

» This study reminds me ...
» A thought God has brought to mind ...
» I want to focus on ...

TODAY'S PRAYER

» Pray that God's unconditional love will pass through you to your teenager.
» Thank God for loving you unconditionally, especially when you didn't deserve it.

NOTES

20
CONGRATULATIONS PARENTS! YOU MAKE A DIFFERENCE

God Speaks . . .
Proverbs 1:8-9

Parents can make a difference in the lives of their teenagers by meeting their teens' needs. Consider these facts:

- Positive connections to parents and family members can protect teenagers from the use of cigarettes, pre-marital sex, drugs, and alcohol, according to a study by the National Longitudinal Study on Adolescent Health. The study also found that "high levels of connectedness to parents and family members" reduced teenagers' distress, thoughts of suicide, and feelings of violence. The researchers also learned that a parental presence in the home, along with shared activities by the teenager and the parents, contributed to many healthy choices by the teenager.[1]
- A report for *Family Relations* defined *empathy* as the "ability to think from another's point of view and to understand another's feelings." Encouragement and praise from parents result in teenagers who are more likely to be empathetic with others. Teenagers who had positive family experiences related better to others and had effective communication skills.[2]

- A study reported in the *Journal of Early Adolescence* found that close relationships with parents result in emotionally healthy teenagers. Most teenagers felt close to their parents, yet retained high feelings of freedom. These youth did not expect their parents to be perfect, but saw them as people.[3]
- A Gallup Youth Survey learned that teenagers look to their parents for decisions that involve the teenager's future and the kind of person that teenager wants to be. In the following areas parents were more influential than peers:

    77 percent of the teenagers say parents are influential on whether or not to go to college;

    70 percent of the teenagers say parents are influential on whether or not to attend religious services;

    66 percent of the teenagers say parents are influential on whether or not to do homework;

    63 percent of the teenagers say parents are influential on what job or career to consider.[4]

The writer of Proverbs realized the value of parents in the lives of their children. A parent's teaching and encouragement is not a burden, but more like a gentle garland of flowers for the head representing wisdom, or a valuable necklace symbolizing the worth of obedience. Becoming a parent doesn't automatically make a person wise. Good parenting comes from watching and copying someone who models good, effective parenting. God, our Father, models the wisdom and understanding for us. We can learn from His Word and from others whom He uses.

TODAY'S CHALLENGE

Make a list of ways you have made a difference in the life of your teenager.

TODAY'S REFLECTIONS

- » This study reminds me ...
- » A thought God has brought to mind ...
- » I want to focus on ...

TODAY'S PRAYER

- » Thank God for the chance to make a difference in the life of your teenager.
- » Ask God to give you wisdom in dealing with the specific situations you will face today with your teenager.

NOTES

_____
_____
_____
_____
_____
_____
_____
_____
_____

21
LOVING UNCONDITIONALLY

God Speaks . . .
Jeremiah 31:3

You can live a life that demonstrates unconditional love, because God loved you first. In Jeremiah 31:3 God says, "I have always loved you" (TEV) and that love continues. When you are loved, you can love.

Unconditional love is a conscious decision of the will to love another person despite how that person looks, talks, or acts. Conditional love depends on "ifs"—"I'll love you IF you don't embarrass me." "I'll love you IF you make good grades." " . . . IF you pick up your room, . . . IF you speak politely to me, . . . IF you don't cause any trouble." A parent who expresses "I love you" only in connection with pleasing actions does not love unconditionally. A parent who shows warmth and concern in an appropriate way to a teenager in good times and in difficult times, whether the teenager looks "strange" or "normal" (whatever normal is for teenagers), whether the teenager seeks that love or doesn't know to ask for it—this parent loves unconditionally.

Although most teenagers don't know what to call it, they know unconditional love when they experience it. It had been a brutal two weeks of up and down emotions and crises in Corey's eleventh-grade year. Every day felt like a battlefield between his parents and Corey. One night at the dinner table Corey lingered after finishing his meal. Only his mother was left at the table. With no prior discussion Corey blurted out, "I'm sorry that the last two weeks have been so bad. Sometimes I don't even feel like I'm in control of what I do. But I do know that you and Dad will love me no matter what happens." Corey's mom told me later that she's glad she didn't say what was going through her mind—*Don't press your luck!* Instead, she was able to hug him and assure him that she and her husband would always love Corey no matter what.

Unconditional love does not mean, however, life without boundaries. In fact, boundaries are a positive part of loving unconditionally. Boundaries regulate behavior in positive ways. Setting boundaries allows your teenager freedom to operate within an acceptable area of behavior. As that teenager matures, those boundaries expand. Smart parents teach their teenagers how to set their own personal boundaries. When boundaries are combined with unconditional love, teenagers are more likely to act responsibly and with confidence. Mary Pipher in her book *Reviving Ophelia* puts it this way, "The ideal family is one in which the message children receive from parents is: 'We love you, but you must do as we say.'"[5]

Loving unconditionally is not easy. You may not be able to love unconditionally all the time—but that's the ideal.

Think of a time when you were loved even though your behavior was inappropriate. How did you feel about receiving that love? How can you express that same love to your teenager?

TODAY'S CHALLENGE

What does your teenager say or do that makes it most difficult for you to love unconditionally? What will it take for you to change your attitude and love unconditionally?

TODAY'S REFLECTIONS

» This study reminds me …
» A thought God has brought to mind …
» I want to focus on …

TODAY'S PRAYER

» Pray that you might be as gracious to others today as God has shown His gracious love to you when you acted inappropriately.

NOTES

22

SIX ASSUMPTIONS THAT GET YOU IN TROUBLE

God Speaks . . .
Proverbs 8:1-9

Assumptions begin with a false premise that is either too broad, too narrow, or one-sided. You get into trouble because you don't look beyond the assumption. Assumptions make it difficult to discover your teenager's real needs. These six assumptions below are not the only false assumptions parents make, but they are some of the most common.

1) *My teenager seems OK; I must be doing everything right.* Many parents refuse to look beyond the surface behavior of their teenagers. As one teenager put it, "I don't lie to my folks. I just don't tell them everything."

2) *My teenager is a mess. I'm a terrible parent. I can't possibly meet this kid's needs.* While the family plays a major role in the life of their young person, they are not the only influence. Other adults, peers, and social pressures push teenagers into unhealthy actions. Don't beat yourself up for all of your teenager's poor choices.

3) *It's just a phase of adolescence. I made it through my teenage years.* A teenager's normal behavior appears abnormal to parents. Be sure you learn what normal developmental behavior includes. Then you are in a better

position to recognize what behavior comes from the developmental process and what doesn't. It's also helpful to understand the culture your teenager lives in.

4) *It's too late* or *It's too early*. It is never too late to work on any relationship. Start today to rebuild a relationship with your teenager.

5) It is never too early. In fact, you have been meeting the needs of your child from the cradle. Some parents think that once this child becomes a teenager, parents don't need to be as involved as they previously were. The amount of attention and importance of meeting needs increases during the teenage years. Parents must stay involved.

6) *My teenager will turn out better than I did.* We all want a better life and a safer world for our children. Most parents wish they could shield their children from the pain and reality of the world, but they can't. They also can't turn their teenager into someone that the teenager doesn't want to be. Wish. Dream. Hope. Pray. Family psychologist John Rosemond reminds us, however: "It's your job to provide good directions; it's your child's job to follow them."

7) *I'm* (select your problem—*a single parent, unemployed, uneducated, an only child, financially strapped, climbing the corporate ladder*), *so I don't have the* (select your excuse—*time, energy, training, money, emotional ability, patience*) *to determine my teenager's needs and meet them.* Parenting is sometimes inconvenient. It can also be a great joy. A long time ago you took on the task of preparing this person for adulthood. Just because the job of parenting can be hard sometimes doesn't mean it's time to stop. You may have to put your needs on hold in order to invest time, energy, and emotions into raising this teenager. (You probably didn't know you signed up for all this when you first became a parent—but, surprise! You did!)

God views assumptions as immature and foolish. Instead of speaking the false beliefs of assumptions, God calls you to be wise, mature, and sensible. Wisdom is straightforward, not twisted by uncertainty or half-truths. Look at Proverbs 8:1-9 and identify ways to avoid making assumptions.

TODAY'S CHALLENGE

Consider an assumption you have about your teenager. Compare the assumption to the facts.

TODAY'S REFLECTIONS

- » This study reminds me ...
- » A thought God has brought to mind ...
- » I want to focus on ...

TODAY'S PRAYER

- » Pray for God to reveal to you the false assumptions that may be hindering your relationship with your teenager.

NOTES

_____
_____
_____
_____
_____

23
A PARENT INVESTIGATOR (P.I.)

God Speaks . . .
Proverbs 22:6

Perhaps the words of Proverbs 22:6 have encouraged you in your parenting. The promise of " . . . and when he is old . . ." may give you hope in view of a rebellious teenager. ("Old" means older than a teenager!) The word *train* is actually the same word used in other places and translated as *dedicate*. By aiding your child's growth, you are dedicating that teenager to the Lord. The next phrase—*in the way he should go*—is crucial. Parents must consider what is best for their individual teenager; each child has a distinct personality that requires parents to react in different ways for different children.

What is a parent investigator? I'm not talking about pulling out your 007 secret identity; this is not about the bad guys versus the good guys. I'm not suggesting you become a spy; that violates the privacy and personhood of your teenager. Neither do you have to be a bloodhound sniffing into your teenager's business. Stay focused on learning the needs of your teenager so you can meet those needs.

An investigator is someone who observes what is going on, then takes the clues and puts them together and figures out the bigger picture. As a P.I., I encourage you to be a keen observer who recognizes the clues that indicate trouble. These clues might include a drastic change in behavior, sudden or unusual secretiveness, different sleeping or eating habits, increasing defiance, withdrawal, problems at school. You are looking for a pattern, not a single instance.

Only if you determine a consistent pattern of negative behavior should you be more aggressive. When you become alarmed about the health or well-being of your teenager, that is the time to act. Be prepared, however, to deal with the consequences. For example, if you search your teenager's room for drugs, know what you are going to do if you find them. Will you confront your teenager? Are you willing to use intervention to get your teenager into a drug rehabilitation program? Are you prepared to send your teenager to a professional counselor? Do you have the name of a counselor?

Be a smart P.I. Be clear on your motives (dedicated to your position as a parent). Be sure you understand normal teenager development and the individual nature of your teenager. Be observant and informed. Be prepared to deal with the consequences—from explaining to your teenager why you were snooping, to handling the problem, if you discover one.

TODAY'S CHALLENGE

Write a statement of your dedication to the role of parenting. Place it where you can see it frequently.

TODAY'S REFLECTIONS

» This study reminds me ...
» A thought God has brought to mind ...
» I want to focus on ...

TODAY'S PRAYER

» Confess your own sins and shortcomings to God before judging your teenager.
» Pray that God will give you eyes and ears that make you a wise, observant, responsible parent investigator.
» If you find a problem, pray for strength and guidance as you make decisions about "the way he should go."

NOTES

_____
_____
_____
_____
_____
_____
_____
_____
_____
_____
_____
_____
_____
_____

24
HOW EMOTIONAL GAUGES WORK: MEETING NEEDS

God Speaks . . .
Galatians 6:7-8

For years, psychologists have identified the connection between thinking, feeling, and behaving. Paul understood this concept too. Negative thoughts result in negative feelings that usually end up with inappropriate or unacceptable behavior. After reading these verses, respond to these statements:

Agree	Disagree	1. Sowing negative thoughts and feelings are a sin.
Agree	Disagree	2. Evil thoughts and feelings cannot bring about good.
Agree	Disagree	3. Positive thoughts and feelings can only result in positive behavior.
Agree	Disagree	4. God is the author of positive thoughts and feelings.

The process of thinking, feeling, behaving is how we get our needs met. If you look beyond the behavior to the thoughts and feelings, you can usually figure out the motivating need. Remember, however, this is not an exact science.

This chart gives you a visual picture of how the thinking, feeling, behaving process ought to work. In these examples the thoughts, feelings, and behaviors build off of the basic gauges. There are unlimited combinations of thoughts and feelings and behaviors, but you can see the vital relationship between this process and meeting needs.

GAUGES	INDICATES CONSTRUCTIVE THINKING	INDICATES FAVORABLE FEELINGS	RESULTS IN APPROPRIATE BEHAVIORS
noticed	My dad pays attention to me.	valued as a person	shows kindness to others
encouragement	My family supports my efforts.	confidence	works to complete a task
empathy	My mom cares when I hurt.	assurance	develops caring relationships with others
direction	I receive praise for my actions.	significant	accepts leadership responsibilities
security	I feel accepted no matter what I do.	loved	treats others politely

Teenagers often confuse feelings with reality. Dr. Mary Pipher in *Reviving Ophelia*, her revealing study of adolescent girls, reminds us that teenage girls are especially vulnerable to "emotional reasoning, which is the belief that if you feel something is true, it must be true."[6] If a teenager feels stupid, he must be stupid. Teenagers further tend to expand "truth" to relate to a period of time that goes beyond the present. If a teenager feels ignored by a parent, she believes her parent will ignore her forever. Feeling and thinking become intertwined in such a way that teenagers often can't distinguish the two. Young teenagers' feelings are intensified by raging hormones and other developmental changes. Most high school students are acquiring the mental ability and the emotional stability to separate feelings from thoughts.

Feelings can overpower thinking. Daniel Goleman, in his book *Emotional Intelligence,* suggests that people were created with two minds—one that thinks and one that feels. He also explains a process that perhaps you have noticed with your teenager, or even yourself. "The emotional mind is far quicker than the rational mind, springing into action without pausing even a moment to consider what it is doing. Its quickness precludes the deliberate, analytic reflection that is the hallmark of the thinking mind. . . . When the dust settles, or even in mid-response, we find ourselves thinking, 'What did I do that for?'—it is a sign that the rational mind is awakening to the moment, but not with the rapidity of the emotional mind."[7]

TODAY'S CHALLENGE

Remember a recent time when you did something totally irresponsible. What thoughts and feelings led up to the experience?

TODAY'S REFLECTIONS

» This study reminds me . . .
» A thought God has brought to me . . .
» I want to focus on . . .

TODAY'S PRAYER

» Pray that God gives you wisdom to see the need beyond the deed.
» Ask God to help you in your thoughts and feelings toward your teenager.

NOTES

25
BECOME AN EXPERT GAUGE READER

God Speaks . . .
Psalm 121

This psalm celebrates the joy of worshiping God. In the psalm the worshiper acknowledges God's concern and involvement in our lives. Circle the words in the psalm about God's faithfulness that encourage you. Consider how these words express a partnership of God with your family in this parenting project.

God's faithfulness supports you as you determine your teenager's needs and become an effective gauge reader.

- If you have my book *Why Your Kids Do What They Do*, ask your teenager to complete the "Needs Evaluation" at the end of chapter 2. Encourage your teenager to mark each need honestly, circling her top three needs.
- Were you aware of the needs your teenager selected?
- What behaviors in the past few months have you noticed that could be linked to the top needs marked by your teenager?
- If you don't have the book, simply talk with your teenager. Explain that you are trying to become a better parent. Share a few ideas about emotional needs. Ask a couple of questions like these to get the discussion started; then listen.
- Tell me about a time when you felt I was unfair or uncaring.

- How did you feel about my failure?
- When you are with your friends, how do you feel?
- When you are with our family, how do you feel?
- What is the most difficult part of being a member of this family? These are tough questions, but encourage honesty. Pay attention to what is not said. Remember, you are listening to discover, not to defend.
- Become an expert on your teenager. Observe what event, action, or response triggers negative behavior. Back away from the teenager's behavior and try to discover the feelings and thoughts that lead to the behavior. Watch the people your teenager wants to be with. What do they offer that attracts your teen? You may want to keep a journal or notebook to note a pattern of behavior. You are not looking at individual episodes of wrong behavior; instead look for a pattern.
- Day-to-day parenting makes it difficult to form a clear perspective. Get another person's perspective. This might be a youth minister, a neighbor, a school counselor, a coach, or a parent of your teenager's best friend. Discuss which needs this person sees in your teenager's life.
- Talk with other parents of teenagers. Find out what behaviors they see in their teenagers and how these behaviors develop. Ask what needs they recognize in their teenagers. Other parents can not only help you distinguish between normal and abnormal behavior, but they can also encourage and support you as you try to keep your teenager's emotional gauges balanced.
- When all else fails, use trial and error. Work through the emotional gauges one at a time, noting responses or changes in your teenager's behavior. This process takes time. Don't get discouraged if you don't see an immediate change. Remember, you may have to undo several years of unmet needs.

TODAY'S CHALLENGE

Write a statement of how the watchful, protective God described in Psalm 121 can help you be an effective gauge reader.

TODAY'S REFLECTIONS

- » This study reminds me...
- » A thought God has brought to mind...
- » I want to focus on...

TODAY'S PRAYER

- » Pray for God's help as you look for your teenager's needs. Ask God to clearly show you—either through your observations, the words of a friend, or your own teenager's words—the unmet needs in your teen's life.

NOTES

_____
_____
_____
_____
_____
_____

26
THE EIGHT MASKS OF TEENAGERS WITH UNMET NEEDS

God Speaks . . .
Psalm 13:1-2

Like the psalmist, teenagers whose needs are not met by parents feel abandoned and forgotten. Unlike the psalmist, teenagers don't know how to express the pain of unmet needs, so they seek other outlets. To get their unmet needs satisfied, they willingly compromise personal morals and convictions to be accepted, to feel approval, to gain the attention denied them by families.

Teenagers put on masks to hide their feelings. They choose these masks unconsciously, but the masks can express the feelings and thoughts of the teenager. Here are the masks I see most often.

Penny the Perfectionist. Teenagers put on this mask to prove themselves to their parents. This masked teenager becomes a perfectionist, compulsive about work and dissatisfied with personal accomplishments. This mask covers up the unmet needs of acceptance, unconditional love, and appreciation.

Explosive Emily. This teenager holds in the pain, hurt, and rejection. Then one day she explodes, spewing angry words and negative behavior over anyone nearby. This teenager doesn't wake up one morning and decide, "Today's the day I'm going to lose it." The explosion just happens. Teenagers in abuse situations may wear this mask, although other situations can cause deep feelings of pain and rejection. This mask covers up the unmet needs of comfort, respect, love, and attention.

Directionless Doug. This teenager lacks direction or purpose. He prefers to hang out in his room, not caring about school, friendships, sports, or other activities. He is unmotivated and feels stuck due to a poor self-image, feelings of insecurity, and little to no confidence. He doesn't believe he has a future because he doesn't believe in himself. He has no concept of what he wants to be or what he wants to do with his life. This mask covers up the unmet needs of direction and purpose, support, and encouragement.

Confrontational Chris. This teenager loves to pick a fight. He's known for attacking others verbally. Debates usually turn into arguments. In some instances arguments end in physical confrontation. Violence or vandalism can be an expression of his anger. He may even join a gang or hang out with destructive friends. As a result, this teenager lacks hope, believing he won't live beyond his teenage years. This mask covers up the unmet needs of encouragement, feeling valued, comfort, and love.

Promiscuous Pete. This teenager chooses sex as a substitute for love. For guys this becomes a sexual contest taken to extremes. For girls it can be a desire to belong to somebody—anybody. Walt Mueller explains this mask this way, "Research has shown that teens will often use sex as a means to express and satisfy emotional and interpersonal needs that have little or nothing to do with sex. Sexual intercourse becomes a coping mechanism to deal with the absence of love and affection at home and a groping mechanism as they grasp at any experience that might fill that void."[8] This mask covers up the unmet needs of love and affection, nurturing, and support.

Jill the Joker. This teenager makes others laugh to get attention. At first, the behavior is funny, but the constant jokes at inappropriate times and the constant demand for the spotlight make it difficult to tolerate this teenager for long. This teenager's parents never look beneath the humor to see the hurting. This mask covers up the unmet needs of attention, respect, value, and appreciation.

Secluded Sally. This teenager uses a mask to withdraw from the world. She sees herself as a victim of life. Everything that happens to her is intentional. Every criticism, correction, or suggestion is spoken to hurt her feelings. She trusts no one. She comes home from school and goes directly to her cave (room). This teenager may not try anything like a sport or going to camp because she believes she will fail. This teenager believes she is inferior because she feels inferior. This mask covers up the unmet needs of respect, appreciation, security, significance, and purpose.

Frank the Follower. A teenager wearing this mask is easily swayed by the crowd. Even though the crowd may change (school, church, ball team), this teenager goes along with whatever they decide to do—good or bad. This mask covers up the unmet needs of acceptance, attention, being valued as a person, and love.

TODAY'S CHALLENGE

Reflect on a mask your teenager might be wearing, why this has happened, and how it can be removed.

TODAY'S REFLECTIONS

» This study reminds me …
» A thought God has brought to mind …
» I want to focus on …

TODAY'S PRAYER

» Pray for God to reveal any masks that prevent your teenager from being open and honest with you.

NOTES

27

RED ALERT

God Speaks . . .
Romans 7:14-25

Do you recognize the behavior expressed in this passage? I do. I get caught in trying to do good and end up doing wrong. Then I try to correct my mistake, and it gets worse. Teenagers may get sucked into a behavior that they've been taught is wrong, yet they have no idea how they got into the mess or how to get out.

The masks you studied yesterday result from a variety of needs and corresponding behaviors, but the same process occurs each time. We discussed the process of thinking, feeling, and behaving earlier. Here unmet needs lead to unhealthy thinking, combined with feelings of pain and hurt, ending in inappropriate, unacceptable, often unhealthy, destructive behavior. Teenagers choose these alternate behaviors to achieve two goals: (1) to avoid the pain of not having a need met; (2) to feel better, connected, loved, accepted by anyone, anywhere. That's the bottom line—to avoid the pain and to feel connected. These teenagers' emotional gauges go on red alert, warning of their unmet needs. The red alert gauges chart is featured below.

RED ALERT GAUGES	RED ALERT THINKING	RED ALERT FEELINGS	RED ALERT BEHAVIORS
unnoticed	My dad doesn't care what I do.	anxious	addictions
discouraged	I always do something wrong.	self-doubt	fails to complete tasks
ignored	No one cares when I hurt.	empty and alone	withdrawal
rejected	I don't do anything worthwhile.	insignificant	can't make friends
insecure	I never feel accepted.	unloved	easily angered

Ross Campbell, in *How to Really Love Your Teenager*, discusses how everyone, especially teenagers, has a unique capacity for emotional needs. He calls it an emotional tank. A full emotional tank indicates needs are being met. A teenager with a full emotional tank ventures into the world to interact in positive, healthy ways. As the teenager expresses independence by going places on his own, by following his peers, by testing the rules and boundaries, his emotional tank empties. If the teenager cannot refill that emotional tank at home, he will look for another filling station.

By reading the gauges, you can tell if your teenager's emotional tank is full. A teenager's negative behavior forces you to look at the gauges and realize that the emotional tank is either empty or has been refilled by others who do not have the best interests of your teenager in mind. Campbell emphasizes the importance of this refilling by the family:

- Teenagers need an ample amount of emotional nurturance if they are to function at their best and grow to be their best.
- They desperately need full emotional tanks in order to feel the security and self-confidence they must have to cope with peer pressure and other demands of adolescent society. Without this confidence, teenagers tend to succumb to peer pressure and experience difficulty in upholding wholesome, ethical values.

- The emotional refilling is crucial because while it is taking place, it is possible to keep open lines of communication between parents and teenagers.[9]

TODAY'S CHALLENGE

Evaluate your teenager's gauges for red alerts that you need to pay attention to.

TODAY'S REFLECTIONS

» This study reminds me …
» A thought God has brought to mind …
» I want to focus on …

TODAY'S PRAYER

» Ask God to allow your emotional tank to be refilled with words of encouragement or signs of acceptance from others so that you can minister to your teenager from the overflow.

NOTES

_____
_____
_____
_____

28

SIX WAYS PARENTS SABOTAGE A RELATIONSHIP WITH THEIR TEENAGERS

God Speaks...
Matthew 18:23-24

Don't be like the forgiven servant who failed to see the relationship between being forgiven and forgiving another. This servant sabotaged his own forgiveness by playing the role of a tough master.

Parents sabotage a relationship with their teenagers by assuming different roles. Often these roles were modeled by their own parents, so the teenager's parents may not know how harmful these roles can be. Other roles may be assumed as a convenience or to hide a parent's frustration, unmet needs, or feelings of inadequacy.

The Nag—This parent substitutes nagging for communication. To stop playing this role, figure out why the teenager procrastinates. Set a time limit on the task to be completed. ("The grass needs to be cut by Friday evening.") Restate the time frame once. ("Today is Thursday. Don't forget to cut the grass by tomorrow night.") If there's no response, the nag can let the request go, decide on reasonable consequences for the child, find someone else to do it, or do the task personally. Nagging can be habit forming.

The Pretender—This parent appears to look good on the outside, but is much like the "Explosive Emily" mask worn by the teenager. Holding in the hurt, anger, and frustration may fool everyone on the outside, but the potential for explosion lies near the surface. This parent can't see the teenager's needs through the veil of suffering sainthood. This parent can't see their teenager's needs due to their own negative emotions. This parent must first determine their own feelings of hurt or pain, then share them with another adult who can listen and comfort.

The Escape Artist—Like an escape artist who sneaks out the back door to keep from being seen, this parent hides behind this role to avoid responsibility. This parent casts blame on others, even the teenager. To stop playing this role, the parent must act like an adult and accept responsibility. If the parent has blamed the teenager for a long time, the parent may need to mend the relationship by offering a sincere apology and asking for forgiveness.

The Spy—The spy or paranoid parent does more damage to a relationship with the teenager than any other irrational parental role. Teenagers know when a parent snoops, and that it comes from a lack of trust. Teens become more secretive as they seek independence from family. But a teenager with a spy for a parent grows more careful and mysterious. Many times paranoid parents drive their teenagers away. This parent usually doesn't have a plan if something wrong is discovered. To stop playing this role, the spy might make a list of fears and worries of what the teenager might be doing and share these with the teenager. This parent must remember to look for a pattern of behavior with supporting evidence before spying.

The Drill Sergeant—This role involves power. Frequently this parent transfers the position of power from the office to the home. Or the parent feels powerless other places and expresses his power at home. This parent won't recognize a teenager's needs until he steps down from his position of power. To quit the commander role, this parent must surrender some power to the teenager, especially as the teenager gets older and learns to make her own decisions. The commander can share the power by offering the teenager two or three options, instead of telling the teenager what to do.

The M.I.A.—This parent is missing in action, being too busy or preoccupied to pay attention to their teenager. Many parents at this time in their lives are at the peaks of their careers and feel compelled to work long hours, leaving little time for family, much less for a teenager. A teenager's busy schedule complicates this relationship. Sometimes the M.I.A. is not so busy, but is unwilling to deal with the teenager. Some parents accept the M.I.A. role because they have no idea how to relate to a teenager. To stop playing this role, this parent may have to make hard choices between career and family, giving the teenager focused attention on a regular basis.

Do you know of other roles parents use to hide their insecurities and shortcomings? Once a parent understands how roles prohibit him or her from recognizing and meeting a teenager's need, that parent can stop playing the role and respond to his or her teen's real needs.

TODAY'S CHALLENGE

Have you played any of these roles? How can you change?

TODAY'S REFLECTIONS

- » This study reminds me ...
- » A thought God has brought to mind ...
- » I want to focus on ...

TODAY'S PRAYER

» Pray that God will reveal roles you play that keep you from relating in a healthy way to your teenager.

NOTES

29
HOW STRESS AFFECTS NEEDS

God Speaks . . .
1 John 4:4

Unusual or unexpected stress can keep a parent from meeting a teenager's needs. Parents in these situations may feel guilty for not meeting their teenager's needs, but occasionally parents must deal with the pressure of heavy stress, especially if it's not long term. Some stress is inevitable in life, but too much stress can harm, even paralyze, relationships. To take a look at how much stress has occurred in your life over the past twelve months, use this adapted version of the Holmes-Rahe scale developed by Dr. Thomas Holmes and Richard H. Rahe at the University of Washington Medical School. Check the events that have happened in your life in the past year.

- ❐ death of a spouse 100
- ❐ divorce 73
- ❐ marital separation 65
- ❐ jail term 63
- ❐ death of close family member 63
- ❐ personal injury or illness 53
- ❐ marriage 50
- ❐ fired from work 47

- ☐ reconciliation with mate 45
- ☐ change in family member's health 44
- ☐ sexual difficulties 39
- ☐ addition to the family 39
- ☐ change in financial status 38
- ☐ death of a close friend 37
- ☐ change in line of work 36
- ☐ change in number of marital arguments 35
- ☐ debt over 10,000 31
- ☐ change in work responsibilities 29
- ☐ son or daughter leaving home 29
- ☐ trouble with in-laws 31
- ☐ outstanding personal achievement 28
- ☐ trouble with boss 23
- ☐ change in work hours, conditions 20
- ☐ change in residence 20
- ☐ change in schools 20
- ☐ debt under 10,000 17
- ☐ change in sleeping habits 16
- ☐ change in eating habits 15
- ☐ vacation 13
- ☐ Christmas season 12

Total the points for each stress factor you checked. Parents with a score of 150 or less are less likely to feel pulled in several different directions. Parents with a score of 150 to 300 have a moderate amount of stress that may be taking its toll in time and energy. Scores of more than 300 mean a family has excessive stress.

Symptoms of a family operating under excessive stress may include

- a general feeling of urgency;
- sharp words, misunderstandings, and an underlying tension among family members;

- a desire to escape—to the bedroom, to the car, or the office—almost anywhere;
- feeling frustrated for not being "caught up" with regular responsibilities;
- not having time for regular, personal care; or
- feeling guilty for not taking care of everyone in the family.

The higher the level of stress, the greater are the chances of a family malfunctioning. Here are several ideas to help bring down the levels of stress:

- identify what causes the stress
- work with the family to find solutions for the stress
- allow the teenager to take on some responsibility, if possible
- involve other people who can help with the work load or offer perspective
- list what needs to be done to diminish the stress, then work through the list
- revise the chores
- focus on the strengths of your family
- find someone outside the family who can listen to your frustration

TODAY'S CHALLENGE

Focus on the verse for today. How does that promise make you feel?

TODAY'S REFLECTIONS

» This study reminds me ...
» A thought God has brought to mind ...
» I want to focus on ...

TODAY'S PRAYER

» Pray for the situation that is causing stress in your life today. Call on God's great power to help you handle this stress.
» Pray for the stress you see in your teenager's life. Ask God to grant your teenager an unusually peaceful day.

NOTES

30
UNMET NEEDS AND FATHERLESS HOMES

God Speaks...
Ephesians 6:4

Over and over, one thing I consistently hear from hurting teenagers is the lack of a dad in the home. Before going any further, let me state how much I appreciate single-parent moms who provide excellent homes for their teenagers and who are meeting their teenagers' needs to the best of their ability. Yet I believe these mothers would agree that not having a dad in the home is a great loss. Here are some of the painful statistics:

- Presently, 40 percent of our children live in fatherless homes.
- Seventy percent of the juveniles in long-term correctional facilities grew up without a father in their homes.
- Children from fatherless homes are twice as likely to drop out of school than children from intact families.
- Drug and alcohol use occurs more frequently in fatherless homes than in homes with both parents.
- Girls who grow up without their father are 111 percent more likely to have babies as teenagers, 164 percent more likely to have a premarital birth, and 92 percent more likely to end their marriages than girls who have a father at home as they grow up.

- The chances of children living in poverty is five times greater for those in fatherless homes.[10]

Walt Mueller, in his book *Understanding Today's Youth Culture*, identifies the fatherless home as one of the greatest disruptions in the lives of teenagers. "We now know that father absence is the greatest variable in the present and future well-being of children and teens. Children who grow through the difficult, challenging, and formative years of adolescence without their dads have a greater risk of suffering from emotional and behavioral problems such as sexual promiscuity, premarital teen pregnancy, substance abuse, depression, suicide, lower academic performance, dropping out of school, intimacy dysfunction, divorce, and poverty."[11]

There is hope as fathers come together to reclaim their roles and to step into their children's lives. Organizations like Promise Keepers or All-Pro Dads are working to equip men to understand the value of accepting responsibility for their homes and children. These organizations give men concrete ways to relate to their children. Some single-parent moms work through their churches or community groups to find male mentors for their sons, but daughters need dads too. Fatherless homes remain a serious problem for the American family.

TODAY'S CHALLENGE

If your home has a dad, be aware of how you might work with a teenager who doesn't have a dad. If you are a single-parent mom, don't become discouraged. Talk to a friend who can encourage you.

TODAY'S REFLECTIONS

» This study reminds me ...
» A thought God has brought to mind ...
» I want to focus on ...

TODAY'S PRAYER

» Pray that God will give you the grace to handle the situation you have in your home.
» Ask for God's peace as you turn toward meeting your teenager's need.

NOTES

_____
_____
_____
_____
_____
_____
_____
_____
_____
_____

31
CONNECTIONS

God Speaks...
John 4:4-27

In the familiar story of the Samaritan woman whom Jesus met at the well, Jesus cut through the shallow relationships perpetuated by customs and society and dealt with the woman's main issue of salvation. He refused to accept the fact that He couldn't talk to her because she was a woman, a Samaritan, had been married five times, and presently lived in sin with another man. Jesus sought a deeper, more significant relationship to connect with the woman.

Relationships form the means through which emotional needs are met. The deeper, more intimate the relationship, the greater the possibility that the need will be recognized and met, helping the teenager function in a healthy way. The less connected, superficial relationships may result in unmet needs.

We usually think of intimacy as the ultimate relationship in marriage, but that same sense of togetherness or connection happens in relationships with others. Deep, intimate relationships develop most often between a husband and wife, parents and their children, and best friends. To achieve this type of relationship the people involved must be willing to be open, transparent, and vulnerable. In fact, here's my definition of intimacy—"into-me-you-see."

It means allowing other people to get close enough that they see your needs, understand your fears, know your weaknesses. As one person in the relationship has a need, the other person recognizes and meets that need.

Superficial relationships, on the other hand, happen in situations where there is less opportunity or desire for closeness. These might be the formal relationships established in a business atmosphere, the casual relationships in neighborhoods, the limited relationships with people whose paths you cross occasionally, such as the teller at your bank or a salesperson in your favorite store. In superficial relationships neither person expects much, so any needs that are met are usually practical, as opposed to emotional or spiritual. Unfortunately, many families settle for superficial relationships.

The lists below define each type of relationship. Circle the words that express how you relate to your teenager at the present time. Based on the number of words circled under each relationship, you can determine the depth of the relationship between you and your teenager.

SUPERFICIAL RELATIONSHIP	AUTHENTIC RELATIONSHIP
indifference	close
formal	personal
careful	caring
factually based	feeling based
controlled	warm
obscure	transparent
distant	together
nonessential	significant
limited	connected
disposable	lasting
comfortable	warm
detached	enthusiastic
weak	constructive
interesting	inspiring
satisfactory	unique

SUPERFICIAL RELATIONSHIP	AUTHENTIC RELATIONSHIP
sympathetic	empathetic
not always available	accessible

TODAY'S CHALLENGE

Look for one way to strengthen the connection between you and your teenager.

TODAY'S REFLECTIONS

» This study reminds me ...
» A thought God has brought to mind ...
» I want to focus on ...

TODAY'S PRAYER

» Pray about your relationship to your teenager. Thank God for the times you have felt really connected. Ask God to reveal additional ways to connect with your teenager.

NOTES

_____

_____

_____

_____

32
RELATIONSHIP SKILL #1—CARING

God Speaks...
John 21:15-17

After His resurrection, Jesus talked with Peter on the shore of the Sea of Galilee. It was a two-fold plan of caring that Jesus shared with Peter. "Simon son of John, do you truly love me?...Take care of my sheep." Do you see it? It took Peter a while too. You can only care for others when you care about Jesus first. As you reflect on caring for your teenager, focus on loving the Lord first.

Healthy, connected, intimate relationships occur when four revolutionary relationship skills are developed and used. As the parent, you can learn to use these skills with your teenager by modeling how these skills improve relationships. Your teenager then learns to use the same skills in relationships with his or her friends. The four skills are caring, trusting, giving, and loving. Each of these will be explained over the next four devotions.

Caring is about putting yourself in the other person's situation and deciding what will comfort, encourage, and support that person. Empathy is a stronger emotion than sympathy. Sympathy says to the teenager, "I'm sorry that happened to you." Empathy cries with the teenager. Empathy takes the deeper step of trying to understand the feelings and thoughts behind the behavior. Empathy does not judge the behavior, but reflects back the pain it hears.

There are many ways to express caring. Caring involves a personal concern for the other person, so you talk about personal topics. Offering both physical, as well as spiritual and emotional, support builds a caring relationship. Tell your teenager you will be praying for him on the day he has a major test. Make an effort to attend the school play your son is in or the debate finals when your daughter participates.

Comfort is most often associated with caring. Comfort your teenager by listening; don't feel like you must have a solution every time.

Affection is the most obvious way to physically express your care. Giving hugs, putting an arm around the shoulder, even your physical presence can be comforting to a hurting teenager.

Measure your caring skills in the relationship with your teenager by completing this caring inventory:

	REGULARLY	SOMETIMES	A LITTLE BIT	NEVER
1. I praise the accomplishments of my teenager.	❏	❏	❏	❏
2. I comfort my teenager when she is hurting.	❏	❏	❏	❏
3. I show affection to my teenager.	❏	❏	❏	❏
4. I express empathy to my teenager for his sadness, his distress, his pain.	❏	❏	❏	❏
5. I support my teenager's healthy decisions.	❏	❏	❏	❏

- In my relationship with my teenager, the ways I show I care are

- One way I could improve my caring skill is_____

TODAY'S CHALLENGE

Notice when someone offers you a caring gesture. Look for opportunities to share a caring gesture with your teenager.

TODAY'S REFLECTIONS

» This study reminds me ...
» A thought God has brought to mind ...
» I want to focus on ...

TODAY'S PRAYER

» Pray for God's continued care over one of your concerns so that you can focus on how to care for your teenager.

NOTES

_____
_____
_____
_____
_____

33
RELATIONSHIP SKILL #2—TRUSTING

God Speaks...
Proverbs 3:5-6

Trust is the major issue between parents and teenagers. Like a barometer, trust measures what's going on in a relationship. The trust level rises when promises and commitments are kept between parents and teenagers. The trust level drops when a trust is broken. If a parent regularly lies to the teenager, that teenager won't trust the parent. If a teenager breaks curfew, the parent's trust level goes down.

The key word for building a trusting skill is *openness*. Trust grows from constant communication of what is expected, then seeing the other person live up to those expectations. Trust is a two-way street. Not only do you need to trust your teenager, but your teenager needs to trust you. Two major enemies of trust are false assumptions and rejection. If a teenager stays out past curfew assuming that "Mom and Dad will understand," his false assumption puts him in danger of breaking a trust. If a parent doesn't keep a commitment to do something with the teenager, the teenager feels rejected.

When trust is broken, your reaction is critical. Do you blow up or simmer? Do you punish immediately or step back and get a broader picture? Was a false assumption made? What information from you will straighten out that false assumption? Was the teenager rejecting you by his actions? Was the teenager feeling rejected? Once a trust is broken, it takes time to restore. Assigning small tasks and seeing results earns trust.

Measure your trusting skills in the relationship with your teenager by completing this trust inventory:

	REGULARLY	SOMETIMES	A LITTLE BIT	NEVER
1. I trust my teenager to make smart, healthy decisions.	❒	❒	❒	❒
2. My teenager trusts me to keep personal secrets.	❒	❒	❒	❒
3. I can be trusted to follow through on my commitments to my teenager.	❒	❒	❒	❒
4. I act in the best interest of my teenager.	❒	❒	❒	❒
5. I share the times and ways I trust God with my teenager.	❒	❒	❒	❒

- In my relationship with my teenager, the ways I show trust are

_____

_____

- One way I could improve my trusting skill is _____

_____

_____

TODAY'S CHALLENGE

Reflect on the verses for today and decide how you regularly trust God.

TODAY'S REFLECTIONS

- » This study reminds me …
- » A thought God has brought to mind …
- » I want to focus on …

TODAY'S PRAYER

- » Thank God for the fact that you can always trust Him.
- » Pray for trust to grow between you and your teenager.

NOTES

_____
_____
_____
_____
_____
_____
_____
_____

34
RELATIONSHIP SKILL #3—GIVING

God Speaks...
Luke 6:38

The reality of giving is best expressed in this verse—"the measure you use, it will be measured to you." When you give much, you receive much. From what you give to God, He returns to you even more, so you can give out of the overflow. That's what God wants to do for you and with you as you build a relationship with your teenager.

Connected relationships depend on giving. In most relationships your meeting another's needs results in that person responding by meeting your needs. Teenagers are a different story. Because they struggle to handle their emotions, to deal with the rapid changes in their lives, to get their own needs met, teenagers will neither be able to recognize nor to meet your needs. You should not expect them to. As the parent you are the primary one to keep your teenager's emotional tank filled. Don't deny, however, that you have needs. Look to God as the primary source of your needs. You can turn to your spouse, close friends, other family members, even your church family as a secondary source to refill to your emotional tank.

Giving to your teenager, however, can benefit you in several unique ways. For example, you might experience feelings of comfort or joy when you are able to help your teen. You can feel encouraged when you see changes in your teenager for the good. You can find hope in watching your teenager grow as needs are met in a healthy way. You can feel grateful for the qualities you see in your teenager. Later, within the strong, connected relationship between an adult parent and an adult child, you may even experience times when your adult child recognizes and meets your needs, but that time is for the future. Presently, you give, and your teenager receives.

As you develop the skill of giving, look for ways to build a relationship between the two of you and the family. Surprise your teenager by doing the unexpected. For example, provide a high-energy snack for a late night of studying, fill your teenager's car with gas, leave a gift card on her pillow for a movie and a meal of her choice. Give by expressing appreciation for your teenager often and openly, as well as to the family and others. As part of the skill of giving, involve him in activities that allow him to give to others, such as feeding the homeless or volunteering at a children's hospital.

Measure your giving skills in your relationship with your teenager by completing the giving inventory:

	REGULARLY	SOMETIME	A LITTLE BIT	NEVER
1. I give focused attention to my teenager on a daily basis.	☐	☐	☐	☐
2. I recognize times of stress in my teenager's life and give encouragement.	☐	☐	☐	☐
3. I include my teenager in times of volunteer service or ministry to others.	☐	☐	☐	☐
4. I express appreciation to my teenager for a job well done.	☐	☐	☐	☐
5. I openly express thanks for all God has given me and my family.	☐	☐	☐	☐

- In my relationship with my teenager, the ways I give are _____ _____

- One way I could improve my giving skill is_____ _____ _____

TODAY'S CHALLENGE

Give something to your teenager that will he a complete surprise.

TODAY'S REFLECTIONS

» This study reminds me …
» A thought God has brought to mind …
» I want to focus on …

TODAY'S PRAYER

» Thank God for giving so much to you, especially the life of your teenager. Pray that God will magnify your efforts of giving.

35
RELATIONSHIP SKILL #4—LOVING

God Speaks . . .
1 John 4:10

The love God gives us reminds us that love is a gift, not a possession. Since He gifted us first, we can gift others with His love.

The final revolutionary relationship skill includes all aspects of love—affection, touching, attention, availability, caring, appreciation. There are so many ways to share love with your teenager. An important aspect of loving is to understand what kind of love your teenager wants and will respond to. Dr. Gary Chapman, in his book *The Five Love Languages of Children,* explains five languages parents use to express love to their children. According to Chapman, your teenager will respond to one love language more frequently than to others. When your teenager's preferred language of love is "spoken," your teenager feels loved. Let me summarize these languages briefly. Perhaps you will recognize your teenager's love language response.

1) *Physical Touch* is given most often to small children in hugs, kisses, and tender touches. When children become teenagers, however, the physical touches may not be as important as the other four languages. Brief touches as you walk past the teenager's chair, a back massage or back scratching, or combing a teenager's hair are all physical ways to

love the teenager who might reject hugs and kisses. Some teenagers, however, enjoy touching and hugging; this language is their primary way of feeling loved.

2) *Words of Affirmation* encourage and affirm the teenager to keep going when times get tough, to hang in there when he feels like quitting. Teenagers who need this language are those who want verbal assurance of the parent's love.

3) *Quality Time* gives the teenager undivided attention for a period of time. Teenagers recognize this language when they feel their parent is available and willing to listen when the teenager wants to talk. The security of knowing the parent is available helps this teenager feel loved.

4) *Giving and Receiving Gifts* is a language often spoken by busy, well – to-do parents who find it easier to give gifts than to get involved in the life of their teenagers. These parents might he surprised to find that some teenagers would rather have quality time or words of affirmation. However, there are teenagers who understand the love behind the gift and see the gift as an expression of love.

5) *Acts of Service* by parents express love through actions that help the teenager. Parents share this kind of love when they work on a car with the teenager, bake the teenager's favorite cake, or help with a science project, for example. A teenager who recognizes these acts of service as special feels loved.

Love can be expressed in many ways. Measure your loving skills in your relationship with your teenager by completing the loving inventory:

	REGULARLY	SOMETIMES	A LITTLE BIT	NEVER
1. I show open, but appropriate, affection to my teenager.	☐	☐	☐	☐
2. I try to make eye contact with my teenager when we talk.	☐	☐	☐	☐
3. I tell my teenager of my love for him/her.	☐	☐	☐	☐
4. I willingly do an activity to show my teenager my love.	☐	☐	☐	☐
5. I give my teenager unconditional love.	☐	☐	☐	☐

- In my relationship with my teenager, the ways I show love are

_____

_____

- One way I could improve my loving skill is_____

_____

_____

TODAY'S CHALLENGE

Notice which love language your teenager prefers, then do something in that language to see the results.

TODAY'S REFLECTIONS

- » This study reminds me ...
- » A thought God has brought to mind ...
- » I want to focus on ...

TODAY'S PRAYER

- » Thank God for His amazing love to you and your family.
- » Pray for God to use you as an instrument of love with your family.

NOTES

_____
_____
_____
_____
_____
_____
_____
_____
_____
_____

36
PARENTING STYLES (PART I)

God Speaks...
Matthew 26:69-75

Peter swore his loyalty to Jesus, then blundered through the late-night events doing exactly what he said he wouldn't do. Perhaps you feel the same sting of pain when your efforts at parenting backfire.

Just about the time you figure out how to relate to an energetic twelve-year-old, you run into the wall of silence that defines a thirteen-year-old. You are always a parent-in-training. Learning how to connect with an ever-changing teenager can be a challenge.

Some parents, however, compound the challenge by making it difficult for teenagers to establish a close relationship. These parents think they are helping when they may be making the relationship more difficult. Three of these ineffective parenting styles are described here. The final three are discussed in the next devotion.

1) *The Rescuer*—This parent damages the parent–teen relationship by not letting their teenager grow up. In an effort to protect, this parent prevents their teenager from experiencing the natural consequences of poor decisions. For example, Dad frequently gives his daughter an extra $20 each time her allowance fails to last through the week. Mom constantly yells at her teenager to get up in the morning, so

he won't miss the school bus. Dad works on his teenager's science project late into the night because his son started too late. Rescuers who continually bail out their teenagers feel angry at their teens for being irresponsible. Underneath, however, rescuers usually fear that their teenagers won't need them any more. Les Christie reminds us that teenagers "should be equipped with the personal strength needed to meet the demands imposed on them by their youth group, school, peer group, and later adult responsibilities. Our goal as parents is for our kids to be truly responsible for their own behavior."[12]

2) *The Passive Parent*—The opposite type of parent from the rescuer is the parent who does nothing. This parent stopped parenting the teenager for a variety of reasons—a personal crisis such as divorce or job loss, being unaware of how to parent a teenager, or feeling burned out by tough parenting problems. The passive parent may live with a more aggressive spouse who takes over the parenting responsibilities. Although teenagers say they want freedom from parents, they don't want parents to go away completely. Teenagers view a lack of involvement as a lack of care.

3) *The Mixed Messenger*—This parent damages the parent-teen relationship by sending mixed messages. I know parents who criticize their teenagers for looking at their phones non-stop but are guilty of texting while driving or scrolling through their emails or social media while eating dinner at home or at a restaurant. What the parent says (her disapproval) and what the parent allows represent opposing messages. Families are not the only ones guilty of sending mixed messages. The media sends mixed messages. (A commercial for sexual abstinence among teenagers runs during a TV movie whose characters end up in bed after the first date.) The schools send mixed messages. (Grades matter most, but if you don't ace the standardized test, SAT, or ACT, kiss your chances goodbye for getting in your

college of choice. Mixed-message parents wonder why they can't get their teenagers to stick with commitments.

TODAY'S CHALLENGE

How did Peter recover from his enormous blunder? What can you learn from Peter's experience that you can use today?

TODAY'S REFLECTIONS

» This study reminds me ...
» A thought God has brought to mind ...
» I want to focus on ...

TODAY'S PRAYER

» Pray for forgiveness if you see yourself in any of these ineffective parenting styles.

NOTES

_____
_____
_____
_____
_____
_____

37
PARENTING STYLES (PART 2)

God Speaks . . .
Ephesians 6:1-4

Let's look at three more types of ineffective parenting styles. These parents think they are improving the relationship between themselves and their teenagers, but they are actually creating confusion and chaos. Do you know parents like this? Have you ever been a parent like this?

- *The Popular Parent*—This parent damages the parent-teen relationship by wanting to he liked by the teenager. He equates parenting with negative feelings and "being friends" with positive feelings. Mom wants a best friend. Dad wants a golfing buddy. But teenagers don't want parents who dress, talk, or act like they do. God established the order of the parent-child relationship (see Eph. 4). The child learns from the parent. These parents may think their relationship with their teenager is healthy until they try to discipline their teenager, and the relationship rips apart. Don't misunderstand—parents and teenagers should be able to share and care, to have fun, to laugh and cry, but you are the adult, the parent, the one providing boundaries, guidance, and love.
- *The Pitiful Parent*—This parent is a variation of the popular parent. As the child grows to look more like an adult, this parent expects an adult relationship. This lonely parent may have trouble relating to

other adults, so the parent depends on the teenager for companionship. Burdened by problems unrelated to the teenager, this parent may expect the teenager to become the parent's priest, hearing confessions of confusion or inappropriate actions, even seeking advice. Tending to be lenient, this parent takes the position of "How could you do this to me?" when the teenager does something that requires discipline. I sometimes see this in single-parent homes where parents live with unusually heavy schedules and little time to develop adult friendships.

- *The Dictator*—This parent desires ultimate control. Rules form the focal point of control. This parent tries to dictate a teenager's every action. This parent destroys communication with dictums and creates rebellion instead of relationship. Dictators don't let the teenager participate in making the rules or in making personal decisions.

There are other parenting blunders that cut communication lines—the embarrassing parent whose behavior, attitude, or addiction is painfully embarrassing to the teenager; the favoritist who openly displays a preference for one child over the other; the explosive parent whose anger can never be understood, anticipated, or controlled; the critical parent who speaks only in words of criticism. These types of parents youth don't want. In contrast Walt Mueller, in *Understanding Today's Youth Culture*, offers a list of what teens want from their parents. Teenagers want:

1) Parents who don't argue in front of them.
2) Parents who treat each family member the same.
3) Parents who are honest.
4) Parents who are tolerant of others.
5) Parents who welcome their friends to the home.
6) Parents who build a team spirit with their children.
7) Parents who answer their questions.
8) Parents who give punishment when needed but not in front of others, especially their friends.

9) Parents who concentrate on good points instead of weaknesses
10) Parents who are consistent.[13]

TODAY'S CHALLENGE

Review the list of ineffective parents and the list of parents youth want and decide which parent you are.

TODAY'S REFLECTIONS

- » This study reminds me …
- » A thought God has brought to mind …
- » I want to focus on …

TODAY'S PRAYER

- » Pray for the willingness and wisdom to develop more characteristics from the types of parents teenagers want than from the types of ineffective parents.
- » Ask God to show you where you blunder unintentionally.

NOTES

_____
_____
_____
_____

38
REVOLUTIONARY RELATIONSHIP BUILDERS

God Speaks . . .
1 John 3:18

I hope you've seen how a vital, dynamic relationship provides the process for meeting needs. You can begin building healthy parenting skills, but it takes time, effort, a knowledge of the teenager's world, understanding his or her development, and cutting through his or her confusion. This checklist provides specific ways to break through the walls and build a relationship with your teenager.

- ❏ Learn how the secular world impacts your teenager. Visit your teenager's school for meetings. Help on registration day or on the first day of class. Know where your teenager goes in the afternoon and on weekends. Listen to the music your teenager listens to; be aware of the YouTube videos they watch or video games they play. What messages is social media delivering to your teenager? What temptations and risks confront your teenager regularly?
- ❏ Look at experiences from the teenager's point of view. What personal stress or anxiety does your teenager feel? Where does that stress come from? Have you met your teenager's friends? What are their concerns, stresses, or problems?

- ❐ Gain an unbiased perspective of your teenager by asking other adults who are around your teenager to assess your teenager's needs. Listen for the grain of truth without defending past mistakes. Use this new perspective to establish a stronger relationship with your teenager.
- ❐ Keep in mind how the rapid changes in your teenager's development influence his or her needs. Unfortunately, numerical years don't indicate emotional maturity. Teenagers are in the process of becoming adults; they haven't arrived yet.
- ❐ Don't wait for their emotional tanks to get too low. Keep refilling through positive strokes. It's been said that it takes eight compliments to make up for the emotional damage done by one criticism. Les Christie reminds us to "look for progress, not simply the finished product. Teens get excited when they know you see them progressing in some good direction.... Don't reward teens for good behavior with food or overly gushy insincere praise. They need to do good because good is good to do. They don't need rewards, they need encouragement. They need feedback. It comes in three forms: compliments, comments, and constructive criticism. You may say, 'This is wrong, but I know you can fix it.'"[14]
- ❐ Father and son psychologists Gary and Greg Smalley encourage parents to "teach our teens—especially daughters—to express [their] needs. This skill can be accomplished by using two questions.

- First, ask your teen: 'On a scale from zero to ten (ten being the best), where would you rate our relationship today?' This question provides a picture of the current state of the relationship.
- The next question, however, is the crucial one: 'What are some specific things Mom or Dad could do over the next week that would move us closer to a ten?' As this question is answered, your teenagers are providing you with the exact things which are needed to improve the relationship."[15]

TODAY'S CHALLENGE

Reflect on the challenging words of 1 John 3:18. Write down an action you need to take with your teenager. Write down a dream you have for your teenager.

TODAY'S REFLECTIONS

» This study reminds me ...
» A thought God has brought to mind ...
» I want to focus on ...

TODAY'S PRAYER

» Pray for God to go before you in building the relationship bridge between you and your teenager.
» If you have a good relationship, ask God to help you make it stronger.

NOTES

_____
_____
_____
_____
_____
_____

39
LOOK IN THE MIRROR AND DISCOVER...

God Speaks...
1 Corinthians 13:11-12

"When I grow up and become a parent, I'll never..."
Do you remember thinking *I'll never do that when I'm a parent?* Are you parenting the way you said you'd never parent?

Do you look in the mirror and see your mother or father? Whether we like it or not, we are products of our past. Perhaps you learned good parenting skills from your parents, but if you didn't, don't despair. Like the familiar verses of 1 Corinthians 13, we see poorly in the mirror at first, then more clearly as we continue to look. Don't be afraid to look in your mirror to the past and learn from it. These next few devotions give you a chance to evaluate your own teenage years and determine if your needs were met or unmet. Here are several basics about your past and parenting:

- *You cannot give what you do not have.* If your parents failed to comfort you over broken relationships or teenage disappointments, or in times of intense stress, you will have a hard time recognizing your teenager's need for comfort. If you don't receive comfort presently from someone in your life, you will find it more difficult to offer comfort to another.
- *You are responsible for the emotional environment in your home.* Your ability to parent effectively depends on creating an emotionally healthy

environment in your home. If the environment where you grew up met your needs, you're more likely to recognize and meet your teenager's needs. If the emotional environment was unhealthy and your needs were not met at home, you may create faulty emotional environment in your home today.
- *You can change.* You can look at the past, take the ideas and actions that worked, throw out the stuff that didn't, and learn new parenting skills.
- *You can develop a more open, honest relationship with your teenager.* By looking at your past and dealing with the pain, you will be able to recognize your teenager's struggles. Knowing what not to do is just as important as knowing what you can do.
- *Your present-day relationship with your parents can develop into a true adult relationship.* You no longer need to feel like a child. You can learn to recognize and meet the emotional needs of your parents as they grow older.
- *You can get your needs met in healthy ways.* As a result, you will be able to relate to others, recognize their needs, and possibly meet their needs in return.
- *You can accept that you are an imperfect person raised in an imperfect environment by imperfect people, but you survived.* You will never be a perfect parent, maybe a pretty terrific parent or a better – than-average parent, but never perfect!

TODAY'S CHALLENGE

Complete the sentence "When I grow up and become a parent, I'll never . . ." Reflect on this statement during the day.

TODAY'S REFLECTIONS

» This study reminds me ...
» A thought God has brought to mind ...
» I want to focus on ...

TODAY'S PRAYER

» Pray for your parents. Thank God (and them) for the sacrifices and struggles they went through to help you become an adult.
» Pray for God's wisdom and insight as you look at your teenage years.

NOTES

40
WHEN I WAS A TEENAGER...

God Speaks...
Luke 6:48-49

In Jesus' story the foundation of one person's life was so shaky that it gave way under pressure. The foundation of the other person's life, however, was set deep and strong. Under stress this foundation held. Today you will look at your foundation and decide how shaky or strong it was.

Begin by looking at your teenage years. Perhaps many of your needs went unmet in your childhood. Your parents had a second opportunity to meet your needs during your teenage years. When needs continued to go unmet, however, you looked for other ways to meet those needs. A search for someone to meet your needs motivated your behavior. Some behavior may have been unproductive, inappropriate, or high – risk. In the space below, list the actions you did as a teenager. For example, you may list *smoking, running with a crowd with different standards than mine, lying to parents, driving too fast, having sex before marriage.* This is your list. No one else will see it, so be honest with yourself. You may have more, or less, than ten.

1) _____
2) _____
3) _____

4) _____
5) _____
6) _____
7) _____
8) _____
9) _____
10) _____

Like teenagers today, you probably didn't recognize your behavior as a consequence of an unmet need. As an adult, however, try to decide on an unmet need you feel was linked to that behavior. Write the need beside each behavior. For example, beside *smoking* you may list *the need to feel significant*, so you tried to take on an adult behavior.

Next, complete the following sentences based on the actions and needs you've studied so far in this devotion. The first set of questions concern your mom; the second set, your dad.

- I remember a time when I most needed my mom to_____ _____and she didn't.
- That made me think that my mom_____.
- That made me feel_____about my mom.
- As a result, I behaved_____.
- The way my mom related to my behavior as a teenager was to_____.
- I wished she had_____.
- Have you ever discussed this with your mom?   Yes / No

    If so, what was the result?_____.

- I remember a time when I most needed my dad to_____, and he didn't.
- That made me think that my dad_____.
- That made me feel_____about my dad.

- As a result, I behaved_____.
- The way my dad related to my behavior as a teenager was to
- I wished he had_____.
- Have you ever discussed this with your dad?   Yes / No

  If so, what was the result?_____

TODAY'S CHALLENGE

Based on these reflections, would you say the foundation in your teenage years was weak or strong? Why?

TODAY'S REFLECTIONS

» This study reminds me…
» A thought God has brought to mind…
» I want to focus on…

TODAY'S PRAYER

» Thank God for getting you through your teenage years.

NOTES

_____
_____
_____
_____
_____

41
MY NEEDS AS A TEENAGER

God Speaks...
Proverbs 3:13-15

Seek the blessings of wisdom and understanding as you search your past to determine your needs and improve your parenting skills.

Evaluate how your needs were met during your teenage years. Remember, you are not accusing or blaming; you are trying to heal. Healing begins when the hurt is faced. In some cases, perhaps one parent met your needs, but the other one didn't. In other cases, you may feel that neither parent met your needs. Others in the family or those outside the family could have satisfied your needs.

Notice that we will use the same needs list we've looked at for teenagers. That way you can see why it may be difficult for you to meet your teenager's need in the present. In the chart below place an "X" by the person or category that expresses who met each need. Don't hurry this evaluation; it is not a timed event. Think back to your teenage years. You may want to look through old photo albums as you remember the needs and relationships in your teenage years.

My Needs as a Teenager

WHO MET THIS NEED IN YOUR LIFE?	MOM	DAD	SOMEONE ELSE	NO ONE
Attention	☐	☐	☐	☐
Respect	☐	☐	☐	☐
Value	☐	☐	☐	☐
Appreciation	☐	☐	☐	☐
Nurture	☐	☐	☐	☐
Support	☐	☐	☐	☐
Comfort	☐	☐	☐	☐
Significance and purpose	☐	☐	☐	☐
Security	☐	☐	☐	☐
Acceptance	☐	☐	☐	☐
Love	☐	☐	☐	☐

- What was your greatest need growing up?_____

_____

- Who met that need most of the time for you?_____

_____

- How did you feel about your unmet needs as a teenager?_____

_____

- From an adult perspective, how do you feel about those unmet needs today?_____

_____

- Most of the time I felt that my mom_____me.
- Most of the time I felt that my dad_____me.

TODAY'S CHALLENGE

Write a letter to yourself about what you felt was missing in your teenage life.

TODAY'S REFLECTIONS

- » This study reminds me ...
- » A thought God has brought to mind ...
- » I want to focus on ...

TODAY'S PRAYER

- » Pray for understanding of an event in your past that brought pain or frustration. Ask God to help you see the situation from a new perspective.

NOTES

42

MY NEEDS AS AN ADULT

God Speaks . . .
Matthew 9:1-8

Jesus recognized the paralyzed man's greatest need immediately, so He forgave the man's sins. That brought criticism from other rabbis. Jesus responded by meeting the man's second greatest need and healed him physically. Determine your needs by asking Jesus to reveal these to you, then accept emotional healing that comes with having your needs taken care of by another.

Just as needs drive your teenager's behavior, the same is true for adult behavior. Most adults usually behave in an acceptable manner. But when they don't get a need met with their first behavior, they may show their real needs through their reaction. Have you ever wondered, "Why did I fly off the handle like that?" "Why did his answer make me so angry?" "Where did that thought (or action) come from?" "I didn't mean to do that!" Behind these surprise reactions are unmet needs.

Write down the primary emotional need you feel is missing in your life today. Here are several examples. I need: to feel appreciated for all I do; to be respected by my children; to feel secure in my marriage; to know someone cares about me; to be accepted even though I'm not perfect; to feel I can share my hurt with someone who understands.

My primary need is_____.

Look at your present needs, using the same gauges you used in evaluating your teenager's needs. Following are the five basic gauges and the related needs. Beside each need write a number from one to ten that indicates how well you feel this need is being met in your life. A "1" indicates the need is not being met; a "10" indicates the need is being met. Take your time as you think through these needs.

The Noticed Gauge

_____I need focused attention that indicates

_____I am respected as a person,

_____valued for who I am,

_____and appreciated for what I do.

The Encouragement Gauge

_____I need to be nurtured as I reach for my dreams

_____and supported when I feel like giving up.

The Empathy Gauge

_____I need to receive comfort when I experience pain, sorrow, or despair.

The Direction Gauge

_____I need to feel a sense of significance and purpose in my life.

The Security Gauge

_____I need to feel physical security,

_____as well as acceptance regardless of my flaws and mistakes

_____and loved no matter what.

Perhaps these gauges don't cover a specific need you have. Great! That means you're thinking. Write the need you feel is missing in your life and assign it a rating here:

_____My need is:_____

Based on the numbers you chose for each need, circle your top three needs (those needs with the lowest rating). From these three needs, select your primary need. This is the one need that deserves immediate attention. Write that need here:

My primary emotional need from this list is_____

_____

How does that match up with the primary emotional need you wrote down earlier?_____

Who do you think can meet this emotional need in your life today?

_____

TODAY'S CHALLENGE

Talk to your spouse, a close friend, or your pastor about this need in your life. Ask for guidance in getting your need met.

TODAY'S REFLECTIONS

» This study reminds me…
» A thought God has brought to mind…
» I want to focus on…

TODAY'S PRAYER

» Pray that God will show you what your primary adult needs are and who can help meet those needs in your life.

43
THE REALITY OF PAST

God Speaks...
James 1:2-4

Being joyful in the middle of a difficult situation is hard to accept. When you look at your past, however, can you see how the difficult event helped your faith mature?

When you think back to your teenage years, do you remember the fun, the good times, the great interaction with your folks? Have you reconstructed a fantasy world of your teenage years? Possibly. Or, was your past so difficult and dark that you prefer to ignore it? Are you willing to look beyond your past fantasies (good or bad) in order to find healing and closure? I hope so. You will not be able to change past events, but you can evaluate the past, find healing from the hurts of the past, acknowledge hope in the positive memories, and work toward making your future better. Use your devotional time today to reflect on the events of your teenage years.

- What was your greatest achievement during your teenage years?
- What was your most difficult experience?
- What was your biggest disappointment as a teenager?
- What person, event, or situation made you angry most often?
- What person, event, or situation helped you laugh most often?

- What is your favorite (or most painful) memory of being thirteen years old?
- What is your favorite (or most painful) memory of being sixteen years old?
- What is your favorite (or most painful) memory of being eighteen years old?
- Who was the most influential person in your teenage years?

Understanding your past makes you more sensitive to and aware of your teenager's present and future. By learning what needs went unresolved in your life, you can recognize what needs are going unmet in your teenager's life. For example, if you felt unappreciated as a teenager, you will not recognize your teenager's need to feel appreciated unless you face the reality of your own lack of appreciation.

Looking at the past may change your relationship with your parents. You won't have to keep your parents in a fantasy position on those parental pedestals. You can let your parents jump down and become real people in your life. You can relate to your parents one adult to another, rather than as a child to a parent.

Looking at your past helps you accept the fact that you are not the perfect parent. Congratulations! Not being perfect means you still need God; it means you still need others.

TODAY'S CHALLENGE

Circle events that resulted in significant growth, either spiritually or emotionally. If possible, discuss these events with one of your parents.

TODAY'S REFLECTIONS

» This study reminds me …

- » A thought God has brought to mind . . .
- » I want to focus on . . .

TODAY'S PRAYER

- » Thank God for the events in your past that helped you grow.

NOTES

44
THE BEST OF TIMES/ THE WORST OF TIMES

God Speaks...
John 8:35

Continue to evaluate your thoughts and feelings about your parents and your behaviors towards them at specific times in your teenage years.

- What is your favorite memory of your dad?_____
  _____

- Why is this event a favorite?_____
  _____

- How did you feel about your dad at the time of this event?
  _____

- How did you act toward your dad at the time of this event?
  _____

- What made you the most angry at your dad?_____
  _____

- What frightened you the most about your dad? _____
  _____

- When were you the most happy around your dad? _____
  _____

- Did you know that your dad loved you? _____
  How? _____

- What is your favorite memory of your mom? _____
  _____

- Why is this event a favorite? _____
  _____

- How did you feel about your mom at the time of this event?
  _____
  _____

- How did you act toward your mom at the time of this event?
  _____

- What made you the most angry at your mom? _____
  _____

- What frightened you the most about your mom? _____
  _____

- When were you the most happy around your mom? _____
  _____

- Did you know that your mom loved you? _____

How?_____
_____

- Which parent took the lead in parenting you during your teen years?

- When you were thirteen which parent made you feel most comfortable?_____Why?_____
_____

- When you were fifteen which parent made you feel most comfortable? _____Why?_____
_____

- When you were seventeen which parent made you feel most comfortable? _____Why?_____
_____

- When you were nineteen which parent made you feel most comfortable? _____Why?_____
_____

- Has any event in your teenage past kept you from a healthy relationship with your parents today?_____
_____

- From your adult perspective of today, what do you think about these events, thoughts, feelings, and behaviors?_____
_____

- Were your feelings in the past accurate?_____
- Were your actions appropriate?_____

TODAY'S CHALLENGE

As you think about relationships in your life, consider the message of John 8:35. We are God's children forever! What relationships do you want to keep forever? Why?

TODAY'S REFLECTIONS

» This study reminds me ...
» A thought God has brought to mind ...
» I want to focus on ...

TODAY'S PRAYER

» Pray that you will be a child worthy of God the Father.
» Pray that you will be a parent worthy of your child.

NOTES

_____
_____
_____
_____
_____
_____

45
CAUGHT IN PARENT TRAP

God Speaks...
Genesis 2:24

Did you fantasize in your later teenage years that someone would rescue you from your parents, marry you, and take care of you forever? A nice fantasy, but not the reality you're dealing with today, is it? Instead of leaving your parents and cleaving to your spouse as Genesis suggests, many adults remain like children to their parents. Are you caught in the parent trap? It can happen in several ways. Here are two.

- Do you revert back to being your parents' child when you return to their home? What things do you do as the child in the family? For example, when my brothers walk into my parents' home, they immediately head for the pantry and the refrigerator to see what there is to eat, even if they've just eaten. "It's a habit," one brother laughs. Or maybe a parent corrects your behavior—"Don't bite your nails." "Sit up straight." "Where are your manners?"
- Do you leave your parents' home resenting their treating you like a child? If you expect a parent to meet an emotional need in your adult life that went unmet in your teenage years, you will be disappointed every time you go home. Let others meet your needs. Learn to enjoy your parents the way they are.

When I go home I continue to be my parent's child because I

_____

- Another way you are your parents' child is by believing the messages they told you when you were growing up. These were negative or positive statements they repeated frequently.

What messages did your parents give you about your physical appearance? ("Aren't you getting a little heavy?" "You can't wear that hairstyle in THIS house!" "It's not what's on the outside, but what's on the inside that counts.")

What messages did your parents give you about your emotions? ("Real men don't cry." "Don't let anyone see how you really feel." "Tomorrow is another day. You will survive!")

What messages did your parents give you about your performance at school, in a sport, through a club? ("Don't disappoint us." "Is that the best you can do?" "I believe in you.")

What messages did your parents give you about your friends? ("Your friends are always welcomed here." "Why do you want to be friends with them?" "You're a good friend to have.")

You interpreted each message through your needs. These messages affected how you thought, felt, and behaved as a teenager. These messages influence your thoughts, feelings, and actions today.

Do you repeat the messages you heard from your parents to your teenagers? Are any of these messages ones you vowed you'd never repeat to your own children? Oops!

TODAY'S CHALLENGE

What can you do to help your parent see you as an adult?

TODAY'S REFLECTIONS

» This study reminds me ...
» A thought God has brought to mind ...
» I want to focus on ...

TODAY'S PRAYER

» Pray for that child inside you that doesn't want to grow up. Ask God to help you gain confidence and let that childish part of you go.

NOTES

46
A TIME FOR HEALING

God Speaks . . .
Ephesians 4:31-32

The steps suggested in this devotion and the next are crucial in the relationship revolution you seek with your teenager.

Step 1—Identify the hurt. You've identified unmet needs in your life in the past and present. Has this been an emotionally painful experience? Has looking closely at your life created other feelings? What has caused those feelings? What hurt did you face in your teenage years? Put that hurt into words.

- The person who hurt me the most as a teenager was _____.
- At the time I felt _____.
- The way I feel about this person today is _____.
- An event that hurt me the most as a teenager was _____
- At the time I felt _____
- The way I feel about this event today is _____.

Step 2—Acknowledge the pain. Don't skip this step. Focus on the emotions behind your pain. Identify those feelings. Involve someone else in your healing. If you are married, talk to your spouse about the situation and people who caused the pain. Ask your spouse to comfort you as you share.

If you are a single parent, share with a trusted adult who will help you deal with your feelings, not try to fix the hurt.

If you don't grieve over this pain, you will remain emotionally tied to the person who caused the pain. Grieving is God's healing way to bring renewal. Without grieving, you keep your emotional tank filled with sadness, anger, hurt—unhealthy emotions that keep out healthier emotions.

Think of a time when you were hurt by something that happened with one or both of your parents. Express your feelings.

- From my_____I missed_____.
- I felt_____about not having this experience with my _____.
- I remember a time when I was emotionally hurt by my_____.
- It involved_____.
- Back then I felt_____.
- Today I feel_____.

Step 3—Gain perspective. Let others help you evaluate your feelings and give a different perspective.

- Talk to siblings about the events that caused you pain. Do older siblings know more of the story? Did they experience similar feelings?
- Ask a trusted family friend or neighbor. Do they know what was happening to your parents that you didn't notice or understand? Did your parents talk to this person and share their feelings about the event? How did your parents describe you to others?
- You may even get a new perspective from your parents. Make a list of actions that you saw as hurtful (*You never came to my ball games. You missed my high school graduation. You always expected me to get an A.*) Beside each hurt write a defense your parent gave at the time or might give now. *[You missed my graduation because you had an emergency business deal out of town that couldn't wait.)* Show the list to your parent, asking if this is a true picture of the situation. Listen to the other

side of the story, not from a child's point of view, but from an adult viewpoint. Does your parent's explanation make sense?

TODAY'S CHALLENGE

Read the Scripture for today. Circle words that relate to your feelings and thoughts. Consider the process of healing.

TODAY'S REFLECTIONS

- » This study reminds me ...
- » A thought God has brought to mind ...
- » I want to focus on ...

TODAY'S PRAYER

- » Pray that God will ease the emotional pain of your past.

NOTES

_____
_____
_____
_____
_____

47
A TIME FOR FORGIVENESS

God Speaks...
James 5:16

1 John 1:9

Continue the steps in this healing process.

Step 4—Forgive and be forgiven. Because God has forgiven you, you can forgive others. You choose to forgive, even though the feelings of pain remain. Forgiving someone who has hurt you gives you strength. Forgive before the person who hurt you asks for forgiveness. Forgive, knowing the person who hurt you may never change his damaging behavior. Forgive even when your natural inclination might be revenge.

To forgive your parent, share your pain with the parent, not in an accusatory, but factual way. You might say, "When I was a teenager, I was hurt when you came home so late that I never saw you. It felt like you didn't like me. I forgive you for that hurt because I want to get on with my life."

If you can't talk directly to your parent without saying the wrong thing, tape record your message. Making the tape lets you edit comments that sound harsh or judgmental. After playing the tape, discuss it with your parent.

Write a letter. Identify the specific incident. If possible, deliver the letter and discuss it. Emphasize that you are not placing blame, just trying to understand and forgive. If your parent has died, letter writing offers a natural release of unexpressed pain. You can also write a letter and not deliver it.

- A hurt I am willing to forgive is_____.
- I am willing to talk to_____about this.
- The way I will do it is to _____.

Be forgiven. Perhaps you need to ask forgiveness from your parents. Your unmet needs may have motivated you to act in destructive ways that damaged your relationship with your parents. After asking God to forgive your sin, ask for your parents' forgiveness.

- A hurt I realize I have caused is_____.
- I am willing to ask forgiveness from_____.
- The way I will do it is to _____.

Step 5—Grow from your experience. Meet the needs of your parents. Perhaps the need is physical in nature, like changing light bulbs or taking care of the lawn. If possible, focus on an emotional need. Maybe your parents need to know they are appreciated, or they would like more attention.

- A need I see in my mom's life is _____.
- I can meet that need by_____.
- A need I see in my dad's life is_____.
- I can meet that need by_____.

In some situations, you should seek professional help. God has gifted others with the ability to give you perspective and to guide you through this tricky emotional stuff. You should particularly seek professional counseling if you are depressed and see no hope, or if you are concerned that you might harm others because of your anger and pain.

Step 6—Thank significant others. During your teenage years, some people did things right. These may have been siblings, other family members, significant adults like coaches, neighbors, teachers, youth workers, even older peers who offered encouragement and guidance. Acknowledge the thanks you owe people who met your needs in a healthy way.

TODAY'S CHALLENGE

Write a note of appreciation to one or two of the people who helped you through a difficult time.

TODAY'S REFLECTIONS

- » This study reminds me ...
- » A thought God has brought to mind ...
- » I want to focus on ...

TODAY'S PRAYER

- » Acknowledge the sins in your life that need forgiveness. Ask God for His forgiveness.
- » Pray that God will help you forgive those who have hurt you.

NOTES

_____
_____
_____
_____

48
MEETING MY FUTURE NEEDS

God Speaks . . .
Luke 10:30-37

You have looked at your past and identified how unmet needs motivated past behavior. The next step is to get your present needs met so you can meet your teenager's needs.

BE AWARE of letting others know your needs. God made us to need one another, so it's OK to ask for help. The first person to consider is your spouse, but don't expect your spouse to read your mind and figure out your needs. Lovingly share your needs in a nonconfrontational way, even if it is your spouse's weakness that leaves you feeling needy. Here's an example of how to share your need with your spouse.

"Honey, I'm really struggling with feeling that my ideas and opinions aren't very important. When there's a decision involving the house or the car or the children, I feel left out when you make a decision without me. Please include me on these decisions in the future."

If you are a single parent, look to other family members and close friends to meet your needs. If your relationship with your parents is healthy, ask them for help. Best friends, siblings, your church family, even extended family can help meet your needs, if they know what you need. For married couples, these are also healthy options.

BEWARE of looking for someone to meet your needs who is inappropriate. You might find yourself caught in an unhealthy situation. For example, if you feel unloved and turn to someone of the opposite sex at work for help, your vulnerability may lead you to make unwise choices.

BEWARE, also, of expecting your teenager to meet your needs. Until your teenager gets emotionally healthy and more mature, he or she depends on you, not the other way around.

BEWARE of whining, acting childish, selfishness, and "pity parties" as you expect others to "discover" your needs. Admitting you have needs is not whining. Whiners complain without seeking or accepting solutions. Childishness sulks and pouts, hoping someone will figure out what's wrong. Selfishness is attacking and blaming others without being truthful. A "pity party" requires everyone to feel sorry for you.

BE AWARE of how you can meet others' needs. You cannot give what you do not have. As your needs are met, it's a natural process to give to others. When your emotional tank is full, start filling the emotional tank of your teenager.

BEWARE of feelings toward your teenager that make it difficult to meet your teenager's needs. Underneath your teenager's "attitude" and clothing and loud music and hair is a hurting person waiting to soak up love, respect, attention, and nurture like a sponge. Attitudes are really shields deflecting the painful reality of life. Clothing and hair are part of the search for individuality. Loud music and strange behaviors affirm that they are still alive. Push past the discomfort of your teenager's strange world and find the reward of helping your teenager.

TODAY'S CHALLENGE

In today's familiar parable, an unexpected person met the injured man's needs. As you evaluate who can meet your needs, consider unexpected people. Perhaps you can be that unexpected person to meet needs in someone else's life.

TODAY'S REFLECTIONS

- » This study reminds me ...
- » A thought God has brought to mind ...
- » I want to focus on ...

TODAY'S PRAYER

- » Pray for God to show you how to ask for help in getting your needs met.
- » Pray that God will show you how you can meet another's needs.

NOTES

_____
_____
_____
_____
_____
_____
_____
_____

49
ABC'S FOR THE FUTURE

God Speaks...
Psalm 51:10-12

This ABCs checklist suggests ways to prepare for meeting your teenager's needs.

- Adjust your attitude. When you understand the reasons behind your teenager's behavior, change from an attitude of frustration and fear to an attitude of confidence. Instead of punishing behavior, become proactive and meet your teenager's needs before the negative behavior starts.

  Have the attitude that sees your teenager as a gift from God. Keep a list of positive qualities you notice each day. Read the list on days when parenting a teenager gets rough. Appreciate what your teenager does right; ignore the rest, if possible.
- Bear responsibility for not meeting your teenager's needs in the past. At an appropriate time, share with your teenager what you are learning. Apologize to your teenager for past mistakes. State your desire to change. ("I have not paid attention to you. Please forgive me. I want to do better. I was wondering if you would like to do something together this week?" or "I didn't know how to he a parent. I've never been the parent of a fourteen-year-old son, but I'm going to try harder. Will

you work with me?") Try to be upbeat and positive when you share your desire to meet your teenager's needs. You may need to repeat this process several times over the next few months in order to discover other neglected needs in your teenager's life.

- Comfort your teenager when appropriate. Working through your own unmet needs showed you the value of comfort. You also saw how not being comforted can hurt. If you were not comforted in the past, you may not know how to comfort others, especially a stricken teenager.

Comforting a teenager requires empathy, gentleness, and affection. Even when a teenager stiffly rejects hugs, a hand on the shoulder or a brief back rub is a comforting gesture. Some teenagers who have not been exposed to comforting words and gestures may enjoy the comforting. Others who are uncomfortable with touching may take a little longer. You also want to weigh how affectionate to be with a teenager based on the comfort level of your teenager with that quickly changing body. Younger teenagers are particularly self-conscious and uncomfortable being close to others. Don't be in a hurry; it may take time for your teenager to volunteer the pain or hurt happening in life. For example, your son may not admit how hurt he is about breaking up with his girlfriend. Your daughter may not know how to explain her embarrassment at changing in the girls' locker room at school. Be prepared to comfort when you notice drastic changes—a vocal teenager who becomes quiet; a restless teenager who becomes listless; an upbeat teenager who acts depressed.

Think of a time when you were really hurting. What words comforted you? What words of comfort does your teenager need? Comforting words sound like this:

"I know this hurts you."

"I'm sad that you have to feel this way."

"I'm here for you."

"How can I help? I love you and want to support you."

Your first experience in comforting your teenager may feel awkward, but the more you do it, the better it will be accepted.

TODAY'S CHALLENGE

A clean heart and a steadfast spirit are what David requested from God. List ways a clean heart and a committed spirit can help you meet your teenager's needs.

TODAY'S REFLECTIONS

» This study reminds me ...
» A thought God has brought to mind ...
» I want to focus on ...

TODAY'S PRAYER

» Pray for a clean heart, a right attitude, and a commitment to the task before you.
» Thank God for the challenge in this task that will continually bring you back to Him.

NOTES

_____
_____
_____
_____

50
DISCOVER, ENERGIZE, FIND, GIVE

God Speaks . . .
1 Peter 1:15

Continue to look at more ABCs as you prepare to meet your teenager's needs.

- Discover the unique nature of each child. Many teenagers complain, "My parents like my brother/sister better!" I realize parents want to treat their children equally, but there is nothing equal about children. The firstborn child ends up with nervous moms and dads who are learning to parent. Finances may be tight. Grandparents watch (and maybe participate) more closely. Children born later arrive into a different financial climate, maybe a different neighborhood with different extended family involvement. As a result, each child's personality and relationship to parents is different.

  Deal with each teenager based on that teenager's strengths and weaknesses. Be especially careful not to project one teenager's negative characteristics on to another child who doesn't have the same emotional makeup. Appreciate the differences in your children.

- Energize your parenting skills. You know you'll never win the "Perfect Parent Award," so try being a really great parent! Using devotional material like this, attending seminars, talking with other parents of teenagers, and learning how they face different situations bring new life and energy to the seemingly endless years of parenting a teenager.

- Find constructive ways to vent the frustrations of life. When you are hurt or angry or tired, call a good friend to listen, jog, shoot baskets, or bang around in the kitchen or a workshop. Never allow yourself to use abusive behavior or language with your teenager. If you feel yourself losing control, or fear you will hit your teenager or use language that tears the teenager down, talk to someone (a trusted friend, counselor, another parent) who can help you get perspective and control.
- Give attention to keeping your marriage healthy. Raising a teenager strains a marriage. The different ways you and your spouse were parented become even more obvious during these years of parenting a teenager. Spend time with your spouse—dinner and a movie, a weekend retreat, a marriage conference at your church. Do something every month that involves just the two of you. This is a tough assignment, but when that last teenager leaves home, you and your spouse want to have something to talk about over dinner. Hopefully, you have included your marriage mate in this quest to understand your teenager. This gives you much to discuss as you work together on helping your teenager.

If you are a single parent, your task is harder, but not impossible. You don't have a soulmate to rely on for emotional and physical support. Enlist a same-sex person who can be a friend, mentor, confidante—someone who can give you perspective and support.

If you currently live in a blended family, then you may already be dealing with the difficult consequences of raising a teenager amid unusual relationships. If you have been a blended family prior to your teenager's adolescence, the impact may not be as great. If you decide to get married during your teenager's adolescence, however, statistics show how traumatic this time is for your teenager. Consider professional help in getting everyone in your new family to work together.

TODAY'S CHALLENGE

Read today's Scripture. Consider ways to be holy in what you do today.

TODAY'S REFLECTIONS

- » This study reminds me ...
- » A thought God has brought to mind ...
- » I want to focus on ...

TODAY'S PRAYER

- » Pray for each family member, identifying a struggle each might have.
- » Thank God for your family and their meaning to you.

NOTES

_____
_____
_____
_____
_____
_____
_____
_____

51
GIVING UNCONDITIONAL LOVE

The ABCs listing ends with "H," hut it is a powerful part of this checklist that is getting you ready to meet your teenager's needs.

- Hold up unconditional love. Although I've discussed the need to show unconditional love in meeting your teenager's needs, I must underscore its importance here. In evaluating your own teenage years, you've seen how conditional love damages, and even destroys, relationships. Unconditional love accepts the person for today—this hour—right now. He is your son; she is your daughter. You gave that teenager a chance at life through birth, adoption, or guardianship. Apart from God, you are the one true source of unconditional love for that teenager.

After reading this passage, grade yourself on these attitudes of love. Mark your responses using this 1 to 5 scale (1 meaning "not me"; 5 meaning "this is me").

___patient   ___kind   ___trusting
___modest   ___humble   ___polite
___detests immorality ___celebrates truth ___never gives up
___faithful   ___hopeful   ___love lasts forever
___protects   ___never fails

Make this Scripture practical. Match the question asked by the parent to the answer supplied by the teenager. Make notes of other ways to answer each question.

The parent asks:

1) What shows you that I am patient?
2) What shows you that I want to be kind?
3) What shows you my lack of envy?
4) What shows you that I don't feel a need to impress you?
5) What shows you that my love is not rude?
6) What shows you that I try to be unselfish?
7) What shows you that I will rarely lose my temper?
8) What shows you that I am willing to forget a wrong?
9) What shows you how sad I am to see you struggle with a relationship or a situation?
10) What shows you my joy when you make a difficult, but healthy, decision?
11) What shows you my desire to keep you safe?
12) What shows you my desire to trust you?
13) What shows you that I have great hope for your future?
14) What assures you that I will always be here?

The teenager answers:

a. when you believe in me as a person with good values.
b. when you listen to my achievements without listing all of yours.
c. when you encourage me in tough times, as well as in good times.
d. when you act nice to my friends.
e. when you respect my privacy and listen to my ideas.
f. when you praise my decisions and help me carry through on them.
g. when you're willing to listen whenever I need to talk.

h. when you offer to pick me up any time of day or night, no questions asked.
i. when you let me live my life without having to pursue your dreams.
j. when you come to my game (drama, debate, or award ceremony), even though you have a lot to do.
k. when you forget the mess I made in the bathroom last week or the way my room looks today.
l. when you won't fight with me even though I try to make you mad.
m. when you're willing to help me with my umpteenth science project, even though you hate science.
n. when you tell me you pray for me.

TODAY'S CHALLENGE

Share this exercise with your teenager. Let your teenager mark the teenage responses. Based on your teen's answers, you can determine which part of your unconditional love needs work.

TODAY'S REFLECTIONS

» This study reminds me . . .
» A thought God has brought to mind . . .
» I want to focus on . . .

TODAY'S PRAYER

» Pray for God's guidance in living unconditional love before your teenager.

52
REVOLUTIONARY RELATIONSHIP PARENTING

God Speaks...
Philippians 2:3-5

Paul challenged Christians to be humble instead of vain, considerate of others instead of ambitious for themselves, and to look out for others, instead of themselves. His ideas went against the traditional way of thinking and acting. They were new, fresh, and revolutionary.

The revolutionary relationship in these devotions is built on understanding and meeting the emotional needs of your teenager. This revolutionary idea goes against the traditional way that most parents parent. Look at this situation, and decide what you would do.

Stuart's grandfather died suddenly. Before his death his grandfather often took Stuart fishing, to the movies, or out to eat good, old – fashioned barbecue. Several weeks after the funeral, Stuart and a couple of his buddies trashed the boys' locker room at school. Stuart was suspended for a week.

Based on the ideas and information you've looked at in this devotional material, would you do something different than what you would have done before this study?

I hope so. I've tried to show you that the way to change a teenager's behavior is to meet needs, not just to react to the behavior. As you think about Stuart's situation, examine the differences of this revolutionary way of relating to teenagers with the way many parents relate to their teenagers.

Many Parents Today...
- focus on the problem behavior
- use punishment as the only way to change the behavior

Revolutionary Relationship Parents...
- look beyond the behavior to the motivation
- meet a need to correct the attitude behind the behavior

Many Parents Today...
- blame others for the problem (peers, society, media, other parents, work)
- operate from frustration
- try to change the teenager when the teenager sees no need to change
- love conditionally ("I'll love you if you stop this behavior.")
- relate to the teenager on a superficial level
- feel uncomfortable because they don't understand the teenager's behavior
- don't have a relationship with the teenager outside of regular disciplinary actions
- suffer parenting burnout
- spend time and energy worrying about your teenager

Revolutionary Relationship Parents...
- accept responsibility for unmet needs and act to meet the need
- operate from confidence
- offer the teenager a reason to change as needs are met
- love unconditionally ("I love you because you are my child.")
- relate to the teenager in many ways

- feel comfortable with the teenager as a deeper relationship develops
- see relationship as the key to meeting needs
- see parenting as a priority until the teenager leaves home
- spend time and energy meeting needs of the teenager

TODAY'S CHALLENGE

Write out a statement of what you hope can be accomplished as a Revolutionary Relationship parent. Keep the statement before you during the day.

TODAY'S REFLECTIONS

» This study reminds me …
» A thought God has brought to mind …
» I want to focus on …

TODAY'S PRAYER

» Pray that you will see success in using the Revolutionary Relationship approach so that you can continue to use this approach.
» Pray for your teenager's day.

NOTES

_____
_____
_____
_____
_____

53
WHAT TEENAGERS WANT

God Speaks . . .
Proverbs 23:24-25

Proverbs points out that teenagers want parents who are delighted to have them as their children.

According to a December 9, 1997, article in *USA Today*, the number one thing teenagers want is happiness. Parents may be surprised to learn that teenagers expect to find happiness in different ways than society expects. Teenagers see financial, personal, and career success as separate goals, not the ways to find happiness.

Teenagers list other "wants" that may surprise parents. A survey of teenagers from twelve years old to seventeen years old identified their wants for a report entitled "Kids These Days: What Americans Really Think About the Next Generation."

- Teenagers want to be disciplined. They aren't. Half the parents interviewed admitted that they fail to discipline their teenagers when they should. One-third of the teenagers agreed.
- Teenagers want encouragement and compliments. Sixty-four percent say they hear positive words from adults nearly every day.[16]
- Teenagers want more attention. Almost half of those polled said they wanted more guidance and attention from adults. Another study

shows that parents spend an average of thirty-nine minutes a week in meaningful conversation with their children.[17] Even if parents count the essential actions of feeding, clothing, reading to, and playing with children from birth through adolescence, their time with the children is still limited. Employed women spend six and a half hours a week in undivided child care; unemployed women spend six hours more. Unemployed and employed men give about the same time of two and one-half hours per week.[18]

- Teenagers want parents' help in making decisions about their future. A Gallup Youth Survey of thirteen – to seventeen-year-olds examined the influence of parents on teenagers' decisions. Parents had the greatest impact on whether or not their teenager attended college (77 percent), whether or not their teenager attended religious services (70 percent), whether or not their teenager did homework (68 percent), and what job or career plans should be considered (63 percent).[19]

TODAY'S CHALLENGE

After looking at this devotion, make a list of what your teenager wants out of life or from you as a parent. How does your list compare to the statistics above? Ask your teenager what he or she wants out of life and discuss their response.

TODAY'S REFLECTIONS

» This study reminds me ...
» A thought God has brought to mind ...
» I want to focus on ...

TODAY'S PRAYER

» Pray for the happiness of your teenager.
» Thank God for the times of rejoicing you've experienced with your teenager.

NOTES

54
WHAT TEENAGERS NEED

God Speaks...
Psalm 131

In several devotions you've looked at the five emotional gauges using the NEEDS acrostic. Starting with tomorrow's devotion, you will find specific actions and attitudes to adopt in meeting your teenager's needs and to keep those emotional gauges balanced. To put these actions and attitudes into effect, follow these steps.

Step 1: Start with a new way of thinking. Approach your teenager's behavior from the new perspective of learning the motivation behind the behavior. That doesn't mean you ignore the behavior. Discipline may be needed in the form of natural consequences or specific punishment. But operate from a proactive, preventive role as you love, encourage, nurture, and respect your teenager into more positive behavior.

Step 2: Focus on one gauge at a time. If you have the book *Why Your Kids Do What They Do,* use the "Needs Evaluation" worksheet at the end of chapter 2 to determine your teenager's most pressing needs. If you have not included your teenager in this process to this point, ask the teenager to take the survey as a way to begin a conversation about needs. Or talk to your teenager about the concepts in this book. Show your teenager the NEEDS acrostic and encourage him to select needs that you can work on.

If you already know your teenager's number one need, focus on meeting that need for the next few weeks.

Step 3: Model what you are trying to do. Model unconditional love. Don't be bullied by a teenager who resists your initial actions. After all, your new behavior and attitude appear suspicious. Don't be surprised if your teenager decides to test you to see how sincere you are. She wants to know if you really are going to respect her privacy, or is this just a phase? He may say or do things to get you to react in your old pattern of behavior. She may act out to see if you really mean "I'm going to love you, no matter what." This testing is normal.

Step 4: Be open about why you are making these changes. Explain that you don't want to repeat the problems you experienced as a teenager when people you counted on didn't meet your needs. Invite your teenager to join you as a partner. Challenge your teenager to give the experience a "test run" of six months.

Step 5: Start today. It's never too late. Stay focused on your goal. Stay in touch with the heavenly Father who wants the best for all His children. Under each gauge are the basic needs. Then you'll find a list of actions and attitudes to use in meeting each need. Some actions can be implemented quickly; others will take time to develop. Use these next pages of suggestions as a workbook. Write in the margins other actions that come to mind. Star or circle the actions you plan to take. Write a date by an action as a time frame indicating when you hope to see a change in your teenager's behavior. Record Bible verses or phrases that come to mind as a reminder that God is in this with you.

TODAY'S CHALLENGE

Today's the day to finally identify at least one need in your teenager's life. Focus on learning that need today.

TODAY'S REFLECTIONS

- » This study reminds me ...
- » A thought God has brought to mind ...
- » I want to focus on ...

TODAY'S PRAYER

- » Pray for your teenager's needs and that you will be sensitive to learning those needs.
- » Ask God for a humble attitude and a peaceful soul that keeps you in touch with Him throughout this process.

NOTES

55
ACTIONS AND ATTITUDES TO MEET: THE NOTICED GAUGE—ATTENTION

God Speaks...
Luke 11:11-13

What do snakes and scorpions have to do with meeting a teenager's need for attention? Attention is one of the greatest needs today's teenagers have. Unfortunately, parents caught in a time crunch, or climbing the corporate ladder, or those who were poorly parented fail to give their teenagers the necessary attention. Instead of receiving "an egg," some teenagers get scorpions. Jesus, however, knew that many parents, even though they are human and have their own failures, want to do the right things. The verses encourage these parents.

The Noticed Gauge—Teenagers need focused attention.

1) Pay attention when your teenager is talking. Watch body language and facial expressions for clues about your teenager's feelings.

- Stop watching TV or turn down the volume when your teenager wants to talk.
- If a discussion is not life-threatening, agree to disagree. Don't argue until someone gets angry or "wins." Remember, your teenager tries out different beliefs and attitudes to see what fits, how others react,

and how the words sound coming from their mouths. Besides, most teenagers can argue both sides of the same issue.
- Say "I'm available," then be available twenty-four hours a day, seven days a week. If it's not convenient at the moment, give your teenager a time frame ("I'll be through in ten minutes. I want to talk with you."). One dad told his secretary to interrupt any meeting when his teenager called.

2) Enter the world of your teenager. Look at events from the teenager's point of view.
- Go to school-sponsored events. Chaperon a church youth trip (with your teenager's permission). Offer to bring food to a fellowship.
- Take a group of young teenagers to get pizza. Let them sit at another table. Listen to their conversations while you drive. Teenagers forget that drivers have ears!
- Watch the TV programs and movies your teenager watches and discuss these.
- Listen to and discuss the songs your teenager prefers. (This is easy to do in a car.) Don't condemn the music. Try to understand why he likes the song, how the music makes her feel, and what message she gets from the song.
- Work on homework together. Show your teenager study shortcuts you've learned. As she explains the subject to you, so you can help, she may suddenly understand the problem. Don't be a "know-it-all"; you can learn something too.

3) Do something special with your teenager.
- Spend time alone with each teenager. Plan a regular (weekly, monthly, bimonthly) "date," if possible.
- Brainstorm a list of activities to do with your teenager. Together select several and write these on the family calendar.

- Let your teenager teach you something (the computer, getting around on the Internet, how to play chess or the guitar, how to program the VCR, the finer points of a sport).
- Explore new places with your teenager (a used clothing store, a bike trail).

4) Indicate what you think about your teenager during the day. Say things like, "I thought about what you said...." "I saw something today that reminded me of you." "A friend at work expressed the same opinion you had about...."
5) Occasionally invite the teenager into your world (for lunch or on an interesting business trip).
6) Eat dinner as a family at least three days a week. Make it a priority. Turn off the TV.
7) Always acknowledge your teenager in the morning, when returning home, or whenever the teenager walks into a room.

TODAY'S CHALLENGE

Choose one action to focus on today.

TODAY'S REFLECTIONS

» This study reminds me ...
» A thought God has brought to mind ...
» I want to focus on ...

TODAY'S PRAYER

» Pray that God will make you more attentive to your teenager.

56

ACTIONS AND ATTITUDES TO MEET: THE NOTICED GAUGE—RESPECT

God Speaks . . .
Proverbs 22:1

The Noticed Gauge—Teenagers want to be respected as persons.

1) Speak with respect to your teenager.
  - Avoid demeaning statements about your teenager as well as insults or derogatory names.
  - Avoid teasing of any kind. Younger teenagers take teasing remarks seriously. Older teenagers feel hassled by teasing.
  - Apologize when you are wrong or when you have hurt your teenager through a misunderstanding, unkind words, unfair discipline, or an incorrect assumption.
  - Praise the way your teenager handles a situation, especially a problem.
  - Don't ask prying questions.
  - If you must correct your teenager, do it privately, away from other children and especially peers. Use a calm tone of voice.

2) Act with respect toward your teenager.

- Respect your teenager's time by being on time. If you pick him up at school or need to get her to an appointment, don't be late.
- Be courteous and use your "company" manners with family members. Say "please" and "thank you."
- Knock before entering your teenager's room or the bathroom when the door is closed. Wait for a response.
- Model the behavior you want from your teenager: speak in a softer voice; let your teenager know where you are going and the time you will return; leave a note when you are not going to be home and indicate the time you will be back home.

3) Respect your teenager's desire for independence.

- Consult with the teenager before committing his or her time to a specific activity (baby-sitting, a neighbor's yard work, a project at church, a youth activity).
- Ask for your teenager's advice or opinion, especially if the decision impacts the teenager (where to vacation, changing schools, how to spend spring break).
- Consider the teenager's need for privacy. If your teenager shares a room with a sibling, figure out a way to give your teenager personal space.
- Do not search your teenager's room unless you have evidence of a continuing pattern that endangers your teenager's health or safety.
- Allow your teenager to have personal time alone with the door shut.
- Understand when your teenager doesn't want to be around you in public; it's not a personal thing, but an independence issue.

4) See your teenager's friends as people whom God loves. Talk to them as teenagers who might be hurting and need someone to listen. Don't stereotype them as weird, even if they are.

TODAY'S CHALLENGE

Write Proverbs 22:1 on a sticky note and place it in a prominent place to reflect on the need for respect.

TODAY'S REFLECTIONS

» This study reminds me ...
» A thought God has brought to mind ...
» I want to focus on ...

TODAY'S PRAYER

» Pray that you will model appropriate respect for your spouse, your teenager, and other family members.

NOTES

57
ACTIONS AND ATTITUDES TO MEET: THE NOTICED GAUGE—VALUED

God Speaks...
1 Peter 2:9

The Noticed Gauge—Teenagers want to be valued for who they are.

1) Value your teenager's positive qualities.

- Frequently say "I think you're a terrific person, because . . ." with specific reasons.
- Applaud your teenager for standing by her morals or showing good character, especially in the face of peer pressure. Slip a note under his bedroom door or send her an E-mail expressing your admiration.
- Support your teenager's healthy, constructive decisions. Verbally applaud wise decisions your teenager makes.
- Talk to your teenager about others' admirable qualities and why you admire them. Ask your teenager to explain why she admires certain people.
- Get in the habit of sincerely complimenting your teenager at least once a day. Compliment the teenager's character, rather than the outward appearance.

- Notice and acknowledge immediately something your teenager does that is positive.
- State how your teenager is a valuable part of the family.

2) Share your admiration for your teenager with others.
- Talk about your teenager's positive qualities to others within the teenager's hearing. Be sincere, not boastful.
- Be positive in what you say about your teenager to others.

TODAY'S CHALLENGE

God values you as a Christian. Look at the numerous titles He bestows on Christians that indicate their value. Think of a title for your teenager that indicates the teenager is valued.

TODAY'S REFLECTIONS

» This study reminds me ...
» A thought God has brought to mind ...
» I want to focus on ...

TODAY'S PRAYER

» Thank God for valuing you as a person and as a Christian.
» Ask God to help you see value and worth in your teenager today.

58
ACTIONS AND ATTITUDES TO MEET: THE NOTICED GAUGE—APPRECIATED

God Speaks . . .
Colossians 4:6

Conversations and actions should be gracious and wise. One gracious action expresses appreciation for what has been accomplished.

The Noticed Gauge—Teenagers want to be appreciated for what they do.

1) State your appreciation.
   - Verbally thank your teenager for completing a task, even if it's a regular chore.
   - Stop expecting your teenager to figure out what needs to be done. Instead, be specific in asking for help and stating a time limit.
   - Volunteer (with the teenager's permission) to chaperon youth events at school or church. Watch and listen to other teenagers during the event. Afterwards, compliment your teenager for something good you saw your teenager do.
   - Praise your teenager in front of others in a pleasant, acceptable manner.

- Catch your teenager doing something right and verbally praise him.

2) Show your appreciation.

- Express your gratitude for your teenager's kindness in a way your teenager will appreciate (a touch, a hug, a thank-you note stuck on the mirror, a flower, a funny card in an unexpected place like her math book).
- Notice what your teenager collects. Occasionally surprise her with a thank-you item for her collection.
- Learn what your teenager likes (candy bar, favorite drink, type of gum). Occasionally surprise him with the item.
- Make a list of the qualities you appreciate about your teenager. Read the list, especially when times are rough.
- Write a prayer thanking God for your teenager.
- Look for things that you appreciate that you can share with your teenager (a cartoon, a starry night, a jogging route).

3) Teach appreciation to your teenager.

- Regularly have a "topic of the day" (news, sports, music, a personal value) at dinner. Agree to disagree with laughter.
- Notice and express your appreciation for God's creation (a beautiful sunset, a rainbow, a new baby).

TODAY'S CHALLENGE

Remember a time when something you did went unappreciated. Be aware of an action by your teenager about which you can express your verbal appreciation today.

TODAY'S REFLECTIONS

- » This study reminds me …
- » A thought God has brought to mind …
- » I want to focus on …

TODAY'S PRAYER

- » Pray that God will make you more appreciative for the little things that happen in life.
- » Tell God how much you appreciate His being in your life.

NOTES

59
ACTIONS AND ATTITUDES TO MEET: THE ENCOURAGEMENT GAUGE—NURTURED

God Speaks...
Romans 12:1-2

Nurturing is a transforming process. Just as God nurtures us as we struggle to become more like Christ, you can nurture your teenager as he struggles to become an adult.

The Encouragement Gauge—Teenagers need to be nurtured as they reach for their dreams.

1) Cultivate the practical side of helping your teenager.
   - Listen to what your teenager struggles with and offer physical, emotional, financial, or spiritual support, as appropriate.
   - Provide financial stability. Don't always talk about how poor you are or what you don't have.
   - Have health insurance for your family. Be sure your teenager carries a health insurance card.
   - Involve your teenager in a project to help others in order to learn the value of service.

- Demonstrate good financial skills by making and keeping a budget, paying off bills, using credit cards responsibly by paying off balances monthly, getting estimates for large projects.
- Teach your teenager how to balance a checkbook, shop for the best buys, use an ATM. By the ninth grade your teenager should have a checking account. Most banks don't charge a monthly fee if the parents have an account in the same bank.
- Go with your teenager to look at colleges. Plan a "college tour" during the summer before his junior or senior year.
- Teach life skills—how to do laundry, how to plan an event, how to shop for and cook a meal, how to iron a shirt, how to make a long-distance phone call, the importance of a credit rating, how to handle emergency situations.
- Involve your teenager in making decisions by weighing the pros and cons, even if the decision does not directly affect your teenager.

2) Help dreams become reality.
- Help your teenager define a life goal.
- Help your teenager set goals for the near future: college, buying a car, paying for prom.
- Allow your teenager to work at a variety of jobs to see what he most enjoys.
- Don't dismiss or discourage a teenager's dreams. Teenagers go from "What I want to be when I grow up" to "How do I get to what I want to be?" If possible, suggest vocational counseling if your teenager is confused or frustrated.
- Assure your teenager of your commitment to her through the long haul.
- Invite engaging adults with a variety of interests into your home to talk about their interests and expose your teenager to other options in life.
- Always hold out hope.

TODAY'S CHALLENGE

Look at the practical skills listed under this gauge. Select one or two to work on over the next few days.

TODAY'S REFLECTIONS

- » This study reminds me ...
- » A thought God has brought to mind ...
- » I want to focus on ...

TODAY'S PRAYER

- » Pray for patience in helping your teenager learn these basic skills.
- » Thank God for dreams that encourage us to reach beyond the ordinary.

NOTES

_____
_____
_____
_____
_____
_____
_____

60
ACTIONS AND ATTITUDES TO MEET: THE ENCOURAGEMENT GAUGE—SUPPORTED

God Speaks...
Isaiah 40:29-31

Read these verses, noting the words that express encouragement and support. Mother eagles fly with their wings outstretched as their babies fly directly above them. Until that baby eagle's wings are strong, the parent eagle remains below. What a great picture of support.

The Encouragement Gauge—Teenagers need to be supported when they feel like giving up.

1) Offer physical support.
- Be action-oriented in supporting your teenager. Support your teenager all the time.
- Post sticky notes with encouraging messages in surprising places—in a school book, on a pet's collar, in his shoes, on her pillow. Send an E-mail with a supportive message.
- Look for funny greeting cards of support to mail to your teenager, especially if you are out of town.
- Walk with the teenager through the normal consequences of poor decisions. (Steven and his friends trashed a church's graveyard one

evening. He felt so bad about the activity that he told his dad. The next day they cleaned up the area together.)

- Do several positive things to encourage your teenager on a really "bad hair" day—leave a sticky note on the bathroom mirror, make a quick phone call of encouragement, treat him to lunch, or have a favorite treat on the kitchen counter when she comes home.
- Celebrate little victories—a completed term paper, the end of final exams, a hard test, or making the team—by fixing his favorite dinner, going out to her favorite restaurant, or doing something your teenager really enjoys, like hiking or biking.
- Do your teenager's regular chores as a way to help out during a difficult time.

2) Offer emotional support.

- Pray for your teenager daily. Tell your teenager you are praying for a specific situation or event. Pray with your teenager in the car (with your eyes open, of course) or over the phone.
- Encourage your teenager to keep a journal of feelings, ideas, statements of anger. Never pry into this journal.
- Notice times of high stress (at midterms, during exams, SAT test days, a family illness), and be especially encouraging and upbeat.
- Never criticize your teenager in front of others, especially peers.

TODAY'S CHALLENGE

Think of someone who has supported you in the past. What made you aware of that person's support? Can you do something similar with your teenager today?

TODAY'S REFLECTIONS

» This study reminds me ...
» A thought God has brought to mind ...
» I want to focus on ...

TODAY'S PRAYER

» Pray for God's support as you become aware of ways to support your teenager.
» Thank God for those who have supported you in the past.

NOTES

61
ACTIONS AND ATTITUDES TO MEET: THE EMPATHY GAUGE—COMFORT

God Speaks...
1 Thessalonians 2:11-12

Paul's words set the stage for the encouraging comfort from an empathetic parent.

The Empathy Gauge—Teenagers need to receive comfort when they experience pain, sorrow, or despair.

1) Focus on the feelings of your teenager.
- Say things that show you care. ("Wow! It sounds like you had a rough day." "I know that was difficult." "I'm hurting with you.")
- Avoid dismissive phrases like "You'll get over it"; "No one ever died of a broken heart"; "Don't make such a big deal of this!"
- Don't immediately place blame. Listen or ask questions to get the whole story.
- Tell your teenager it's OK to cry. Cry with your teenager, but don't use your tears to manipulate your teenager.
- Recognize that teenagers have feelings, too, even when they can't express them. You might ask, "Doesn't this make you angry?" "I'd be frustrated; aren't you?"

- Be aware of how devastating certain events can be in your teenager's life: rejection, disappointment, a physical illness or surgery that isolates the teenager, stress (real or imagined), unemployment (firing), the death of a person (grandparent, favorite relative, another teenager), the death of a pet, a national or local tragedy, parents' divorce, a move, any broken relationship.
- Apologize for bringing sorrow and pain into your teenager's life for whatever reason—divorce (even if it happened when your teenager was young), a business move that uproots your teenager, caring for an elderly parent—whatever the stress is.

2) Help your teenager deal with the pain, hurt, or crisis.
   - Listen without offering a solution. (Dads, even though it is our nature, we don't have to solve the problem every time.)
   - Hug your teenager during a rough time, or put a hand on her arm or your arm around his shoulder to show your concern.
   - Cheer up your discouraged teenager by spending time together in an activity that the teenager enjoys—movie and a pizza, a ballgame, putt-putt golf, playing a computer game.

3) Apologize when you are wrong.
4) Don't talk about your bad day or your bad experience unless your teenager asks.
5) Make your teenager's friends feel comfortable in your home. Hang around the kitchen while your teenager's friends are in your home; teenagers always want to eat! If they stay in the den, bring them soft drinks and popcorn.

TODAY'S CHALLENGE

Empathy goes beyond saying, "I'm sorry this is happening." Empathy takes on some of the pain. How have you experienced empathy? Notice times when an expression of empathy would be appropriate during your day.

TODAY'S REFLECTIONS

» This study reminds me ...
» A thought God has brought to mind ...
» I want to focus on ...

TODAY'S PRAYER

» Pray that God will make you a more empathetic person.

NOTES

_____
_____
_____
_____
_____
_____
_____

62
ACTIONS AND ATTITUDES TO MEET: THE DIRECTION GAUGE— SIGNIFICANCE AND PURPOSE

God Speaks . . .
Jeremiah 29:11

The Direction Gauge—Teenagers need to feel a sense of significance and purpose in life.

1) View your teenager as important.
   - Find out what makes your teenager feel significant—verbal or written praise, praise shared with others about your teenager, encouragement on a task, working with your teenager on the task—then do it.
   - Practice seeing life from your teenager's perspective.
   - Write your teenager's activities on the family calendar.
   - Remember dates of significant events—graduations, getting the learner's license and driver's license, SAT test days, exams, senior prom, awards ceremonies, games.
   - Attend games, recitals, concerts, award programs, school dramas, church presentations—all activities that involve your teenager.

2) Help your teenager discover purpose.

- Introduce your teenager to a variety of opportunities and situations. Support a teenager's desire to try out for the team or to be on the debate team or to try drama or karate.
- Expose your teenager to a variety of entertainment, from live theater to art displays. Make a list of all the events in your area and plan with your teenager to do something different each month for a year.
- Pray for your teenager's strengths and weaknesses, for gifts and abilities, and for your teenager's future mate. Let your teenager "catch you" in your time alone with God.

3) Teach your teenager about being important.
- Lead your family in a home Bible study. Talk about the promises in the Bible, the passages on love, the characteristics of God, the miracles of Jesus, the Proverbs, what we mean to God.
- Involve your teenager in opportunities to see the servant side of life. For example, send your teenager on youth mission trips. Do a missions project as a family (serve in a local soup kitchen, participate in an Angel Tree, volunteer at a local hospital or inner-city recreation center, build a Habitat house together).
- Talk about news stories, events, and situations where other people care for, give to, and serve others.
- Model that others are significant by treating everyone with respect and kindness. Don't use racial slurs or prejudicial terminology about people from other cultures, economic situations, or religions.
- Encourage your teenager's desire to make a difference in life.

TODAY'S CHALLENGE

Write a paraphrase of today's Scripture on an index card that you can stick in your pocket. Let the words make you aware of how the God of all creation is personally involved in your life and the life of your family.

TODAY'S REFLECTIONS

- » This study reminds me …
- » A thought God has brought to mind …
- » I want to focus on …

TODAY'S PRAYER

- » Thank God for His blessings of having a plan for your life and giving you a hope for your future.
- » Thank God for making you aware of the significance of your teenager.

NOTES

_____
_____
_____
_____
_____
_____
_____

63
ACTIONS AND ATTITUDES TO MEET: THE SECURITY GAUGE—SECURITY

God Speaks . . .
Isaiah 60:18

It's going to take a God-sized act to make our neighborhoods and schools and community areas safe again from the growing violence of evil. But God made this powerful promise to Israel!

The Security Gauge—Teenagers need to feel physical security.

1) Offer physical safety.
   - Create a physically safe home.
   - Work with school officials, law officers, other parents, and neighbors to make your teenager's school and neighborhood safe. Find out what safety precautions are in place at your teenager's school.
   - Treat your teenager in a healthy manner. Never threaten your teenager. Never hit or throw anything at your teenager.
   - Acknowledge your teenager's fears. Listen as your teenager talks about these fears.
   - If possible, provide a cellular car phone for driving teenagers. Ask your teenager to call you when leaving a function to come

home. State your expectations about the use of the cell phone. (For example, no long distance calls unless the teenager is out of the area; no talking on the phone while driving; no calls over three minutes; use of the phone only for emergencies.)
- Tell your teenager to call you for a pickup no matter the time, place, or circumstances—no questions asked! This could be from a party, after a ball game, from a friend's house, at the mall. The situation might involve alcoholic beverages, being threatened by another person, being stalked at the mall, feeling rejected by the others, feeling unsafe. If it is not practical for you to pick up your teenager, offer to pay the taxi fare.
- If you can't be home when your teenager gets home, make a thirty-second phone call a couple of times during the afternoon to let your teenager know you care. Try to have an interesting comment or statement to share, not "just checking." Vary the times of the calls.

2) Establish and defend family values.
- Clarify family standards and your expectations about things like curfew, driving, riding with another teenage driver, clothing, chores, language, friends in the teenager's bedroom, TV use, videos, music, parties, spending money, outside school activities, and other areas of a teenager's life. Do not assume that your teenager knows your position on any of these.
- Renegotiate family standards frequently, especially as the teenager becomes older and shows he can be trusted. Tell your teenager you are willing to talk about these issues anytime.
- Discuss how to set personal boundaries. Let your teenager know the boundaries you place in your life. (For example, if you travel, what restrictions do you place on yourself? How do you decide

what movies to see? What activities do you do or not do away from the family?)
- Defend your teenager's boundaries when others try to violate them. Tell your teenager, "Make me the bad guy!" That way the teenager can say, "My dad will explode if I do that."

3) Demonstrate the security of your marriage.
- Assure your teenager of your marriage commitment. Live out this commitment by the way you and your spouse treat one another.
- Keep disagreements with your spouse between the two of you. Don't involve your teenagers either as messengers or pawns. Don't manipulate your teenager into taking sides in an argument with your spouse.
- If you are single, put your teenager's needs first, waiting until the teenager has become an adult before remarrying.

4) Demonstrate a desire to trust God, especially in times of uncertainty or danger.

TODAY'S CHALLENGE

Walk through your home today and evaluate the physical security of the place. Mentally walk through your teenager's typical day and evaluate the physical security of the place where your teenager goes.

TODAY'S REFLECTIONS

» This study reminds me …
» A thought God has brought to mind …
» I want to focus on …

TODAY'S PRAYER

» Pray for the physical safety of your home and family.
» Pray for the moral safety of your family.

NOTES

64
ACTIONS AND ATTITUDES TO MEET: THE SECURITY GAUGE—ACCEPTANCE

God Speaks . . .
Luke 17:3-4

Jesus discussed the need to forgive and accept another person, even if it occurs over and over. Every person desires acceptance. If a person doesn't find it from a healthy source, he will turn to an unhealthy source.

The Security Gauge—Teenagers need to feel acceptance regardless of their flaws and mistakes.

1) Focus on the teenager.

- Accept the teenager, even when the action is unacceptable. Say, "I'm still going to love you even though I do not like what you did."
- Focus on major issues; ignore minor ones. Ask yourself what you can ignore (even though you may not like it) including hairstyle, clothing, condition of the bedroom. Focus on areas that are more important such as attitude, values, attendance at school and worship.
- Regularly ask for your teenager's input on what to fix for dinner, what to do over the weekend, where to go for a Saturday outing. Adopt the teenager's good ideas.

- Avoid favoritism among siblings. While parents cannot love equally, they can love unconditionally. Find something you like about each child (a character trait, not a physical trait or ability).
- Do not refer to your teenagers by negative or stereotypical nicknames ("the smart one," "our jock," "the baby").
- When your teenager has been rejected by another, be understanding; don't lecture. Say something positive like, "That guy's gonna wake up someday and realize how sorry he is not to have someone with your compassion in his life."
- Don't compare the performance, ability, or characteristics of one teenager to a sibling, another teenager, or a parent.

2) Forgive and forget your teenager's negative behavior.
- Let your teenager know that failure is not final.
- Quickly forgive your teenager for something the teenager has done to hurt you, even if your teenager doesn't ask for forgiveness.
- Notice when failure or disappointment happens in your teenager's life and respond by listening.

TODAY'S CHALLENGE

Notice how others' body language (crossed arms, leaning forward or away from the other person, placing a barrier between the two people, smiling and nodding, frowning) expresses acceptance or rejection. What do you do unintentionally that expresses rejection instead of acceptance of your teenager?

TODAY'S REFLECTIONS

» This study reminds me …
» A thought God has brought to mind …
» I want to focus on …

TODAY'S PRAYER

» Pray for God's grace in understanding how to accept the person without accepting the action.

NOTES

_____
_____
_____
_____
_____
_____
_____
_____
_____
_____
_____

65
ACTIONS AND ATTITUDES TO MEET: THE SECURITY GAUGE—LOVED

God Speaks . . .
Romans 12:9-13

The Security Gauge—Teenagers need to feel loved no matter what.

1) Begin with a loving attitude.
   - Stop thinking about your teenager in critical or negative terms.
   - Develop inside family stories and jokes where a key word or a signal tips off other family members. Do not choose a story or joke about the teenager, however.
   - Regularly evaluate your willingness to love your teenager, "no strings attached."
   - Love with God's gracious (undeserved), unconditional (not based on action), unlimited (never runs out) love. Be as gracious to your teenager as God is to you when you mess up.

2) Put love into action.
   - Show affection in physically appropriate ways—a hug, a back rub, a pat on the back, a wrestling match, by playing one-on-one basketball.

- Always say "I love you" as your teenager goes out the door for the day, when you drop your teenager off somewhere, at night when your teenager goes out or goes to bed, and at the end of a telephone conversation.
- Make eye contact when talking with your teenager.
- Find out what love language (see "Relationship Skills #4—Loving" page 76) your teenager prefers, then use that language often.
- Develop the habit of daily conversation. It doesn't need to be deep, just regular. Talk in a place where your teenager feels comfortable, not trapped. (For example, talking in the car is easy because both of you are looking forward, although some teenagers may feel trapped in a car.)
- When you get angry, speak softly or call time out until you calm down. Don't let conflict escalate into degrading or harmful words or actions.
- Hold hands when you pray at a meal.
- Be spontaneous. Occasionally show love for your teenager by doing something unusual—breakfast in bed, an unbirthday celebration, a surprise trip to a favorite sports event.
- Laugh at yourself, at unexpected events, at something your teenager thinks is funny, but never at your teenager's actions, unless your teenager laughs first.
- Listen without interrupting when your teenager is talking. Don't start thinking about what you need to say to your teenager; just listen.
- Be transparent and vulnerable. Share when you need a hug (don't drag out all your problems; just let them know you need love too).

TODAY'S CHALLENGE

In today's verses, circle the words related to love and loving. Express your love for your teenager in an unusual or unexpected way today.

TODAY'S REFLECTIONS

» This study reminds me…
» A thought God has brought to mind…
» I want to focus on…

TODAY'S PRAYER

» Pray that you will become more aware of God's great, gracious, unconditional love. Ask God to let that love flow through you to your teenager.

NOTES

_____
_____
_____
_____
_____
_____

66
ARE YOU WILLING TO CHANGE?

God Speaks . . .
2 Peter 1:5-9

Look at the progression of characteristics mentioned in these verses that improves your understanding and relationship with Jesus Christ. Which of these characteristics would improve your understanding and relationship with your teenager?

For the past several devotions you have looked at specific needs with actions that help you meet the needs of your teenager. As you read through those actions, what have been your thoughts?

"I already do this."

"What's so new about these ideas?"

"No one can do all these things!"

"These would be perfect things to do in a perfect world, but my teenager will never go for these ideas."

"I've already tried. Nothing works."

Most of us use emotional reasoning—our feelings—to decide what actions to take and what to avoid. Emotions can give false information that keeps you stuck where you are. Essentially, you're saying one of the following:

I can't change.

I won't change.

I don't know how to change. (I'm helpless.)

I would change if things were different. (It's hopeless.)

I tried to change and it didn't work.

Don't ask the wrong question—"Can I change?" Ask the right question—"Will I change?" If what you're doing today isn't working, what happens if you change?

Have you ever stood in your teenager's room at 2 a.m., looking at an empty bed, and wondering "Where could she be at two in the morning?"

"What is she getting into at this time of night?" Are you afraid for your teenager's safety? Do you feel guilty for not doing "the right things"? Are you angry at her defiance? Does frustration take over, so that you usually attack your teenager when she finally walks in the door?

What would happen if you hugged your teenager when he got home? How would he feel if you stated that you were glad he was home safely? What would happen if you told your teenager you care about him without attacking his being late? What would happen if you apologized to your teenager for the time your home is legitimately a difficult place for your teen to be?

You cannot make your teenager change. You can, however, change the environment, your attitude, your actions, and your relationship. Then stand back and watch your teenager respond to the change.

Will you change?

TODAY'S CHALLENGE

Don't get stuck in an attitude that is not open to change. Think about all the areas of your life that have changed in the past six months. Today look for ways to change that are healthy and keep you growing.

TODAY'S REFLECTIONS

- » This study reminds me ...
- » A thought God has brought to mind ...
- » I want to focus on ...

TODAY'S PRAYER

- » Pray that God will make you more flexible and willing to try different ideas.
- » If you already feel comfortable with change, then ask God to show you areas in your relationship with your teenager that need the most change.

NOTES

_____
_____
_____
_____
_____
_____
_____
_____
_____

67
REVOLUTIONARY INSIGHTS

God Speaks...
Deuteronomy 31:30—32:4

Moses prepared the Israelites for his death and for the transfer of his leadership to Joshua. The poetic language of this portion of the song draws a vivid word picture. Moses' basic ideas reminded the people to follow God. Many of the ideas I've shared with you are basic, but I pray that they will "fall like rain" and inspire new attitudes and actions in your relationship with your teenager.

Prior to studying these devotions, how would you have handled your teenager's anger? Would you have fired back with loaded words and louder arguments? Hopefully, you realize your teenager's anger is a symptom of a neglected need. You now understand the need to listen to your teenager's anger and empathize with the emotion as you uncover the motivation behind the anger. You can utilize specific actions to meet the missing need. This is true for any action that your teenager does—lying, talking back rudely, drinking, breaking curfew, speeding, whatever.

Identify one revolutionary idea you've learned that has changed your behavior toward your teenager.

- A behavioral problem of my teenager involves_____.
- The way I have dealt with the situation in the past was_____

- The new way I've learned to deal with this problem with my teenager is to_____

What insights have you gained in these specific areas?

OLD WAY	AREA	NEW WAY
	My attitude toward my teenager	
	The way I discipline my teenager	
	The way I relate to my teenager	
	The way I express unconditional love	
	The way I communicate with my teenager	

As an interested, involved parent you can change the way you relate to your teenager. With time and effort you can improve damaged relationships and restore broken ones.

Here's a summary of these revolutionary insights.

- All people have needs. Teenagers' needs are complicated and heightened by their developmental processes.
- Needs motivate your teenager's behavior. When needs are met in a healthy, loving way by parents or other significant adults, your teenager is more likely to respond with positive, healthy behavior. When needs go unmet by parents or other adults who could offer positive support, your teenager may look to unhealthy, destructive sources to get their needs met.
- Looking beyond the behavior to the feelings and thoughts behind the behavior helps a parent discover unmet needs.

- The five gauges (noticed, encouragement, empathy, direction, security) provide a base for determining your teenager's needs.
- Correcting the behavior of your teenager may include facing those unmet needs. Correcting your teenager's behavior can be a learning opportunity, especially if your teenager is allowed to face the natural consequences of the behavior without parental intervention.
- Meeting needs begins with unconditional love and grows from a connected, intimate relationship between the parent and teenager.
- You cannot effectively meet your teenager's need unless that need has been met in your own life.
- Meeting a teenager's needs can prevent problems from occurring, as well as heal problem behavior that has already taken place.
- Meeting a teenager's needs is proactive, rather than passive, parenting.

TODAY'S CHALLENGE

What one concept has been a revolutionary idea? How have you used that concept in your relationship with your teen?

TODAY'S REFLECTIONS

» This study reminds me ...
» A thought God has brought to mind ...
» I want to focus on ...

TODAY'S PRAYER

» Pray that God will continue to make you aware of your teenager's emotional needs.

68
OUT-OF-TOUCH PARENTS

God Speaks...
James 1:5

Ginger is thirteen years old. "When I was younger, my mom checked on me all the time after I got home from school. The phone would be ringing as I walked in the door. Now, she says I'm old enough to take care of myself. She doesn't know about the other kids coming over. I clean up before she gets home. It's pretty fun being in charge of my life!"

Eighteen-year-old Becky writes, "My parents leave for work before I get up. Then I usually have a club meeting or a practice after school. We haven't eaten a meal together since last Christmas. I bet if we sat down to eat together, we wouldn't have anything to talk about. They don't know what happens in my life. I don't think they care."

Many parents today are out of touch with their teenagers. They've lost touch because they fail to communicate. Teenagers tell me they want to talk to their parents, but their parents are too busy or lack interest. Parents tell me they want to talk to their teenagers, but teenagers never stay home, and when they are at home, they retreat to their bedrooms. Unfortunately, parents tend to talk at their teenagers, through their teenagers, about their teenagers, but never talk with their teenagers. The results look like this.

The 27th annual survey of Who's Who Among American High School Students found these differences in what parents thought and what teenagers did:

DO YOU KNOW IF YOUR TEENAGER HAS...	PARENTAL MYTH	TEENAGER REALITY
contemplated suicide?	9%	26%
cheated?	37%	76%
had sex?	9%	19%
friends with drug problems?	12%	36%
driven drunk?	3%	10%
worried about pregnancy?	22%	46% [20]

A recent survey by Partnership for a Drug-Free America found similar results:

DO YOU KNOW IF YOUR TEENAGER HAS...	PARENTAL MYTH	TEENAGER REALITY
tried marijuana?	21%	44%
been offered drugs?	38%	60%
friends who smoke pot?	5%	71% [21]

By now you know that the motivation behind a teenager's unproductive behavior is an unmet need. But the discrepancy between reality and what a parent believes is happening indicates that help is needed in communicating needs. You won't be able to meet your teenager's needs unless

1) you know what the need is;
2) you can communicate to your teenager your desire to help;
3) your teenager responds to your efforts.

In the next few devotions you will see ways to speak clearly and listen intently so that misunderstandings and conflicts don't undo your best intentions of meeting your teenager's needs. You don't have to be an out-of-touch parent.

TODAY'S CHALLENGE

How would you have responded to the two surveys? Which remarks at the beginning of this devotion might relate to the feelings and experience of your teenager? Why?

TODAY'S REFLECTIONS

- » This study reminds me ...
- » A thought God has brought to mind ...
- » I want to focus on ...

TODAY'S PRAYER

- » Pray for wisdom to know your teenager. God promised it in James 1:5, so you can ask for it.

NOTES

_____
_____
_____
_____
_____
_____

69
SIX COMMUNICATION BLOCKERS

God Speaks...
Proverbs 15:4

See how the two ways of speaking explained in Proverbs relate to parents who intentionally or unintentionally block communication with their teenager.

"If you tell your mom the truth, she's not going to listen to it like a friend would. She's going to be looking out for you. Like, 'Hmmmm... Maybe you shouldn't stay out that late.' And, 'Maybe you should be hanging out with a nicer crowd that will read on a Saturday night.'"

Justin has a point. If parents could listen without talking and react without going overboard, teenagers might talk more frequently and less superficially with their parents. But parents fresh from years of controlling the conversation suddenly face a sulky, less talkative teenager—and it goes downhill from there. When a teenager does talk, parents can be their own worst enemies. The first step in improving communication is to identify and avoid the following communication hindrances.

The Reporter states the facts truthfully, but does nothing to discover the teenager's feelings. Teenagers react to life with their feelings. Their perceptions color reality. While statements of logic or fact may be useful in another context, in a conversation with a teenager facts minus feelings bring conversations to a halt!

The Criticizer critiques every part of the teenager's behavior. Normally, parents can observe a teenager's actions, passing on helpful information in a positive context to promote growth and maturity. The criticizer, however, blames the teenager first before getting all the information. This parent's reaction may be tied to other factors unrelated to the problem (an offensive hair color, unusual clothing, past behavior). An aggressive criticizer may even use derogatory names, put-downs, or inappropriate teasing. Criticism ends conversation quickly.

The Martyr plays a game of one-upmanship. No matter what the young person faces, the martyr always creates a more personal, "I'm – worse-off ' scenario. This communication blocker can be hard to identify because the martyr hides behind the excuse, "I'm just sharing my experiences too. Isn't communication a two-way street?" This argument works with adults. In communicating with teenagers, the teenager needs to be the focus.

The Resistor refuses to acknowledge the problem. This parent acts indifferently to the teenager's problem, perhaps not responding at all. A variation of this communication blocker is the one who leaves a room in a heated discussion. These parents fail to connect with their teenagers because they resist facing the reality in their teenagers' lives.

The Anticipator already has an answer as soon as the teenager starts talking. This parent anticipates the teenager's thoughts, feelings, and reactions, interrupting the teenager to express these thoughts. As a result, this communication blocker doesn't listen at all. Coincidentally, the teenager of this blocker parent doesn't talk at all.

The Fixer-Upper has good intentions, but the outcome doesn't help a teenager prepare for life in the real world. As soon as this parent hears pain, frustration, discouragement, or any number of negative emotions, he launches into ways to fix the situation. No project is too small; no cost is too great. Whatever it takes, this parent plows ahead, ready to correct the situation, leaving the teenager successfully stripped of the ability to figure out her own solutions.

To avoid being a communication blocker parent, look at the experience from your teenager's point of view. To learn your teenager's emotional needs, stay in touch with your teenager's emotional world. While parents see a bigger picture, remember the narrow focus of the world of teenagers. In this narrow world every action is critical; every emotion, a crisis. In the next devotion I share ways to overcome these communication blockers.

TODAY'S CHALLENGE

Listen to your conversations with your teenager today. Do you sound like one of the communication blocker parents?

TODAY'S REFLECTIONS

» This study reminds me ...
» A thought God has brought to mind ...
» I want to focus on ...

TODAY'S PRAYER

» Pray for God to make your conversation one that is healing and helpful.

NOTES

70
ARE YOU LISTENING? TECHNIQUE #1

God Speaks...
James 1:19

We are a society of listeners. We listen to the news in the morning and rush-hour reports in the afternoon. We walk into a room and click on the TV or radio to dispel the silence. We listen to reports at work, listen to others on the phone, and listen to neighbors at the mailbox. Even in worship we listen to music, prayers, meditations, Scripture readings, and sermons. Rarely do we enjoy the silence. All this listening drowns out what we really need to hear—each other.

Think about your last conversation with your teenager when you really listened. (Don't count the two sentences you said to your daughter about her curfew.) What was the main topic of the conversation with your teenager? Who initiated the conversation? Who did most of the talking? What was the result, outcome, feelings, or expectation from that conversation? How could the conversation have been improved?

Listening is a learned skill. James 1:19 reminds us that God made us to be listeners first (two ears) and talkers second (one mouth). Eugene Peterson's biblical translation called *The Message* draws a graphic word picture of this verse—"Lead with your ears, follow up with your tongue, and let anger straggle along in the rear." Somewhere along the way, many parents reverse the order of listening and talking.

In fact, the University of California, Santa Cruz recently assembled several studies on parent-child communication, finding out that moms and dads communicate differently to their children. Moms are more talkative, use praise, agreement, and approval more often, yet tend to be more critical than dads. Dads are more likely to give suggestions, state opinions, and ask more questions.[22] All that talking—who's listening?

I'd like to suggest nine techniques for listening to your teenager. You probably do some of these. Let these help you think of other ways to improve as a listener.

1) *Reflect back what you hear.* Paraphrase what you hear your teenager say. You can use phrases like, "As I understand it, what you're saying is . . . "From what you tell me, I gather . . . "Listening to what you've said so far, . . ." This indicates that you are listening. WARNING: Using your teenager's identical words sounds childish and condescending, and comes across as Psychology 101. No teenager wants to feel like he is being grilled by a shrink.

Here's an example of how to reflect what you hear, using the teenager's statement about school from yesterday's devotion.

Teenager: "I hate school. Every teacher has it in for me. I can't do anything right. I wish I could quit."

Reflective Parent: "OK, let me get this straight. Something happened today at school that made you mad."

Additional techniques are presented in the next few devotions.

TODAY'S CHALLENGE

Find an opportunity to use this technique today with your teenager.

TODAY'S REFLECTIONS

- » This study reminds me ...
- » A thought God has brought to mind ...
- » I want to focus on ...

TODAY'S PRAYER

- » Pray that God will give you an opportunity to listen and learn today.

NOTES

71

ARE YOU LISTENING? TECHNIQUES #2, #3, #4, AND #5

God Speaks...
Ephesians 4:29

Continue examining the techniques that help you listen to your teenager.

2) *Clarify by asking questions.* You may have to ask several questions before you get the whole picture. Don't jump to conclusions or offer advice. You've already seen how that stops a conversation. If possible, use the questions to move the teenager to discover his own conclusions. Let's continue with the example started in yesterday's devotion.

Teenager: "Yeah, every teacher had it in for me today!"

Clarifying Parent: "What happened? Which teacher are you talking about?"

Learn to ask questions that address feelings too. You help your teenager express his feelings by stating the potential feelings you hear. You also help your teenager learn to express her feelings by sharing your feelings about her problem. A feeling response encourages further conversation. Feeling questions and responses sound like these:

"Wow! You must be really angry."

"How frustrating! What happened?"

"It makes me sad to see you so depressed. How can I help?"

Once your teenager hears you express your concern, an explanation follows. But even if you don't get a further explanation, you have affirmed your interest in your teenager through the language of feeling words.

3) *Listen with your eyes.* Watch your teenager's nonverbal signals. I've heard many times that communication is only seven percent verbal; the rest is communicated by the speaker's body. Is your teenager's facial expression tense, sad, dark, or glaring? Is her skin color flushed or sallow? Are the teenager's gestures nervous or agitated, like kicking a leg or wringing hands? Is the teenager's posture slumped or erect? Are his arms crossed over his chest or flailing the air? Is her breathing shallow and fast or heavy and labored? What tone of voice is involved—angry, sarcastic, silly, gentle? If you will be still and watch, you will hear more than is spoken.

4) *Listen when they want to talk.* Every parent knows how teenagers tend to pick the worst moments to want to talk. Through some strange phenomenon a teenager's mouth loosens in direct proportion to the lateness of the hour. Whether your daughter comes in from her date ready to share her day or your son stays up late to watch TV, then remembers he wants to ask you something; these are the times that parents must be available to talk. The day is coming when you can sleep through the night. Don't miss these valuable moments of reflection and recharging. Consider these treasured moments when you acknowledge how important your teenager is to you through your focused attention.

5) *Listen with courtesy.* Treat your teenager with the same respect and kindness you would show a friend. Do you talk to a friend in loud, angry words? Do you interrupt, jump to conclusions, or offer unsolicited advice? Do you assign blame quickly? Let your demeanor reflect your respect.

Don't hurry when talking with your teenager. When asking questions, allow time for your teenager to form an answer. Most parents don't realize that as mental development occurs in teenagers, communication skills drop. Teenagers frequently search for just the right word. They struggle with placing their thoughts into spoken words. They use the wrong words and get confused easily. I was counseling a young teenager one night when he finally shook his head and announced, "Rodney, I wish my parents could just read my mind!" Give your teenager space and time to think through what she wants to say. Don't try saying it for him unless it's in the reflective, clarifying mode of "Are you saying . . . ?"

TODAY'S CHALLENGE

Which technique could you use today?

TODAY'S REFLECTIONS

» This study reminds me . . .
» A thought God has brought to mind . . .
» I want to focus on . . .

TODAY'S PRAYER

» Pray that your words today may build up your teenager.

NOTES

_____

_____

_____

72
ARE YOU LISTENING? TECHNIQUES #6, #7, #8, AND #9

God Speaks . . .
Matthew 10:16

Today you finish the nine techniques designed to improve your listening skills with your teenager.

6) *Listen with your touch.* Let your body language show your interest. As you listen, move closer to your teenager, if you think this will encourage your teenager to continue talking. Say your teenager's name in a positive manner during the conversation. If appropriate, place your hand on your teenager's arm or shoulder. Acknowledge his feelings with simple words or phrases like "Oh," "I see," "Wow!" "Mmm." Sometimes words aren't even important.

One mother walked into her kitchen late one afternoon to start dinner and found her twelve-year-old daughter crying at the kitchen counter. Without saying a word, the mother gathered her daughter in her arms and held her until the weeping stopped. She offered her daughter a tissue as the girl headed toward her bedroom. The mother never learned the reason for the tears.

7) *Listen with wisdom and innocence.* Parents need to "be as shrewd as snakes and as innocent as doves" (Matt. 10:16) as they communicate with teenage children. Be wise about the world of teenagers. Know the temptations they face every day. Don't assume it's not happening to your kid. At the same time, don't assume the worst of your teenager without a pattern of behavior. Be innocent as you listen and learn. If you keep an open mind and don't jump to conclusions, you have a better chance of understanding your teenager. One young person put it this way: "Between the 'hey, how's it going' kind of thing and 'so tell me all about your life and how I can fix it,' there's a fine line."

8) *Listen by example.* Communicate in the same manner that you want your teenager to talk with you. Speak in a pleasant voice. When you get angry, avoid sarcasm, red-flag words that create additional feelings of anger, name-calling, or useless threats. Listen when the other person talks. Don't interrupt conversations on the telephone. Don't listen to conversations on the telephone. Keep your prejudices and stereotypes out of the conversation. Be comfortable with the fact that you and your teenager can disagree and still talk to one another. Above all, live your life consistently with what you say. Teenagers may not hear all you say, but they watch everything you do.

9) *Listen with courage.* Talking with your teenager is tough. You never know where a conversation will lead. You want to know what's going on in his life, but you may hesitate to learn the truth. It takes courage to listen without having the final word, but by doing so you let your teenager grow up. It takes courage to listen without offering advice, but you help your teenager learn how to make decisions.

One way to be courageous is to say "yes" as much as possible. Think about all the "don'ts" teenagers hear in their world. If your teenager asks for something, be courageous and see if there's any way you can say "yes." Weigh the positive response with the possibility of building trust and maturity.

Listening is a painful, joyful, enlightening, confusing, discouraging, fun, hopeless, and hopeful adventure. As you listen, you may experience the same range of emotions as your teenager feels. But if you remain determined to meet your teenager conversationally, one day you may hear, "Thanks for being there when I needed to talk. I could always count on you."

TODAY'S CHALLENGE

Of the nine techniques, which do you do best? Which do you do poorly? Decide what you will have to do to be a better listener.

TODAY'S REFLECTIONS

- » This study reminds me ...
- » A thought God has brought to mind ...
- » I want to focus on ...

TODAY'S PRAYER

- » Thank God for His willingness to listen to you when you pray, anytime, anyplace, for anything. Ask Him to make you that willing with your teenager.

NOTES

_____
_____
_____
_____

73
FIVE STEPS TO REDUCING AND RESOLVING CONFLICT

God Speaks...
2 Samuel 12:1-11

No matter how well you communicate, conflict happens between parents and teenagers. Handle the conflict of tomorrow by considering your options today. Your goal is not to have winners and losers, but strong relationships and respect.

1) *Confront the problem quickly.* Conflict occurs over just about anything—misunderstandings, hurt feelings, lack of attention, unfair treatment, false accusations, even a casual conversation that develops into an argument. Perhaps you hurt your teenager by being abrupt or self-absorbed. Your teenager may have hurt you with unkind words. If left unresolved, bitterness, broken trust, fear, guilt, or anger can damage the relationship. As soon as you realize there is a problem, deal with it.
- Go directly to the teenager. Although you may talk to your spouse about the problem, don't expect your spouse or another child to get involved if the conflict is between you and your teenager.
- Attack the problem or the hurtful action, not the teenager ("I love you, but I don't like your tone of voice or your words").

- Call "time-out" if the conflict gets heated. Do NOT walk away without an explanation that this is a time-out; set a time to continue. ("We're getting too angry. Let's take ten minutes to cool down, then try again.")

2) *Maintain your self-control.* Remember, you are the adult in the relationship, and you need to stay in control. Do not get down on the level of an immature teenager.
- Don't take the bait. Teenagers are notorious for knowing how to push parents' hot buttons. They can say something ("You don't really care about me!") that we feel needs defending ("I do care.
- That's ridiculous."), and the argument begins. Instead, say in a calm voice, "I'm not going to fight with you."
- Use "I" messages rather than the accusatory "you" messages. Your teenager immediately turns defensive when the sentence begins with "You did …" "You should have …" An "I" message starts with your feelings or how you are affected—"I am hurt.…"
- "I'm concerned about …"
- Admit your failures and mistakes. Ask for forgiveness.

3) *Show concern through your response and reaction.* Reduce the tension and conflict by speaking in a calm voice with carefully thought-out words. Use the listening skills you learned earlier. Maintain eye contact so your teenager can see your concern and willingness to listen.

4) *Work out a compromise.*
- Make a list of all options. Eliminate those ideas that aren't practical or safe. Decide on the options to consider.
- If you get stuck trying to think of options, start a new thought line by asking, "Have you thought about …?" or "What would happen if you …?"
- If you have reached a stalemate and can't come up with a solution, involve a third party. Choose someone who is acceptable to you

and your teenager—an uninvolved, disinterested person like another parent, a youth minister, or a family counselor—who can hear both sides and help you reach a compromise.
- Do not accept compromise in areas that are illegal, dangerous, or too risky for a teenager. For example, it is never acceptable for a teenager to drive drunk, take illegal drugs, or break the law in any way.

5) *Cultivate the relationship.* Even after conflict has occurred, be quick to forgive or to ask for your teenager's forgiveness. If the conflict is not completely handled, continue to talk about the problem until it no longer bothers either of you. Don't let anything become a barrier between you and your teenager.

TODAY'S CHALLENGE

Notice how Nathan handled the conflict with King David. He did it privately. He laid out the problem in a calm, factual manner. He was direct in making his point. What can you learn from Nathan's confrontation with David?

TODAY'S REFLECTIONS

» This study reminds me ...
» A thought God has brought to mind ...
» I want to focus on ...

TODAY'S PRAYER

» Pray for a calm spirit and an openness in settling any conflicts that arise today

74
WHAT TO DO WHEN YOUR TEENAGER WON'T TALK (PART 1)

God Speaks . . .
Romans 8:26-27

God provided the Holy Spirit to help us when we don't know what to say to God in prayer. In the same manner, when your teenager doesn't know what to say, don't feel shut out. Use your abilities to figure out what is going on. Let the Holy Spirit guide you here too.

As teenagers gain independence, they tend to turn to friends for conversation and advice. Even when teenagers know their parents want to talk and are willing to listen, talking to parents feels like they have to give up hard-earned freedom and independence. Don't panic! Nontalkative teenagers "happen" to all families.

If your normally chatty teenager suddenly becomes sullen, secretive, or withdrawn, look for a variety of causes beneath your teenager's silent surface. Stress at school or in a sport or with friends creates an emotionally drained teenager who is worn out physically and emotionally. A teenager who feels guilty or ashamed is usually not going to be very talkative. Perhaps the young person must deal with anger or hurt. Or your teenager may fear your rejection or your judgment and punishment without having a chance to offer a fair explanation. Some teenagers don't want a parent's advice, so they never mention the problem. A few teenagers are lazy and haven't learned how to talk with others.

Both parents and teenagers may develop advanced cases of selective hearing, choosing to respond to only what they want to hear. Poor communication skills keep younger teenagers from expressing their feelings. Some young people think their parents don't care, are too busy, didn't want to have them as children, don't know what's going on in the real world, or don't know how to help, so the teenager never makes the effort to talk. Others stop talking if a parent betrays a trust. I've had many teenagers complain that their parents repeated their secrets to friends and neighbors.

The following ideas may increase your chance of conversation with your teenager; however, there are no guarantees. Pick and choose what might work for you. If it doesn't, try another approach.

1) *Create a listening environment.* Commit to a time for daily conversation. Dinner offers a great time to talk about events. Unfortunately, about 20 percent of today's teenagers never eat a meal with their parents. Encourage open doors in your home. Be willing to turn down (or off) the TV. Share activities (like walking or searching the Internet) or chores with your teenager.

2) *Try "parallel conversation."* Although most communication experts say to look a person in the eye when talking to him or her, teenagers are different. They are more likely to talk when you aren't looking at each other. For example, talk in the car where both parent and teenager watch the road. Parallel conversation can also happen while working in the yard, shooting baskets, jogging around the track at school, shopping at the mall, even watching TV together. In parallel conversation the emphasis is on the activity; the talking is incidental.

3) *Ask for your teenager's advice.* Let your teenager help you think through a problem. ("I have to give a speech tomorrow on the number one problem among teenagers in America today. What do you think that is?" "How can I get my third-graders interested in math? You like math; what would you do?") If your teenager asks you about one of her problems, don't offer advice too quickly. After gathering the facts, ask the teenager what she wants to see happen. Toss around the pros and cons.

You'll find more ideas in tomorrow's devotion.

TODAY'S CHALLENGE

Notice how people around you include others in their conversations. How can you draw your teenager into a conversation?

TODAY'S REFLECTIONS

- » This study reminds me ...
- » A thought God has brought to mind ...
- » I want to focus on ...

TODAY'S PRAYER

- » Pray that God's Spirit can help you understand your teenager.

NOTES

_____

_____

_____

75
WHAT TO DO WHEN YOUR TEENAGER WON'T TALK (PART 2)

God Speaks . . .
Galatians 6:9

Here are a few more ideas for trying to get your teenager to talk.

4) *Use forms of communication other than verbal.* A young friend of mine says, "Talking makes my ears tired." I agree. Sometimes we don't hear because we can't listen anymore. Communicate in other ways.

- Written messages give a unique importance to the information. Sticky notes make it possible to leave brief messages in creative places to surprise and encourage your teenager. Slip a computer-generated thank-you note or a letter of admiration under your teenager's bedroom door. Write a letter of support to your teenager before a difficult event or when she faces a major decision. If you're uncomfortable talking to your teenager about a topic, write a letter. If you need a response, make out a checklist or other brief reply for your teenager to send back to you. Send E – mails to your teenager, if you have a computer.
- Tape-record (audio or video) a message. Leave an audiotape on the dashboard of the car with an affirming message on crucial days like the day of the prom, the SAT, a major presentation at school, the

final game of the season, or graduation. Ask a question at the end of the tape that encourages the teenager to continue the dialogue with you later.
- Save cartoons or funny sayings from the newspaper or a calendar. Write on it "What do you think?" and tape it to the bathroom mirror.

5) *Wish along with your teenager.* Listen for what your teenager dreams, then wish with your teenager. Your teenager knows when you can and can't grant a fantasy, but saying things like, "I wish I could make it go away," "I wish you could live today over again too," "I wish we had the money to get a better car," "Wouldn't it be fun to take off for the beach today?!" lets the young person know you understand those feelings of longing. Besides, it's always fun to dream out loud!

6) *Ask effective questions to get responses.*

AVOID "How was your day?" "What did you do today?" "How's it going?" These don't require much comment from the teenager.

ASK: If you really want to know, build off an event that was supposed to happen that day to the teenager. Your teenager may be surprised you remembered. "How did you feel about your speech today? How did the other teenagers respond?"

AVOID any question that can he answered with "yes," "no," or a grunt! Teenagers are notorious for responses like "I dunno," "It's not my problem," "Yeah."

ASK questions that are open-ended, that call for an opinion or feeling, that uncover new information. Open-ended questions allow the teenager to express both thoughts and feelings. Questions might be:

"What led up to that?"

"What did you do then?"

"How do you feel about the situation?"

AVOID "Why?" questions that put the other person on the defensive. "Why did you do that?" These types of questions sound like you doubt the teenager.

ASK "What?" and "How?" questions that tend to provoke more response. Combine these with encouraging phrases like "Go on..." "I'd like to know what happened."

7) *Take what you can get.* Talkative teenagers who become nonresponsive may want a little more independence. If you work to keep those communication lines open, your teenager will return to talk to you another day.

TODAY'S CHALLENGE

Consider how today's Scripture can encourage you as you communicate with your teenager.

TODAY'S REFLECTIONS

» This study reminds me ...
» A thought God has brought to mind ...
» I want to focus on ...

TODAY'S PRAYER

» Pray out loud for a specific situation your teenager faces today.

76
WHEN THEY SAY WHAT THEY NEED, ARE YOU LISTENING?

God Speaks...
Proverbs 25:11

Practice listening to your teenager with an awareness of his needs. Occasionally a teenager may say, "I need a hug!" but most of the time the message is more oblique. Use these commonly spoken phrases to determine what your teenager might need. Two or three needs can go with each phrase. There are no right or wrong answers. Write down phrases you hear from your teenager and decide which need is involved. The needs are:

THE NOTICED GAUGE	THE ENCOURAGEMENT GAUGE	THE EMPATHY GAUGE	THE DIRECTION GAUGE	THE SECURITY GAUGE
attention	nurtured	comfort	significance and purpose	security
respect	supported			acceptance
valued				loved

1) "You don't care what happens to me."
2) "My head hurts."
3) "Did you notice that I put gas in the car yesterday?"
4) "Is anyone going to be at my game tonight?"
5) "Doesn't anyone knock around here?"
6) "This is too hard."
7) "I forgot to mow the lawn; sorry."
8) "Nobody's going on that old retreat; why do I have to go?"
9) "I mess up every time."
10) "I can't wait to get out of here for good!"
11) "I didn't get the job."
12) "Nobody showed up but me."
13) "I can't be your perfect child!"
14) "What were you and Mom fighting about last night?"
15) "I hate my hair."
16) "Don't expect me to bring home all A's."
17) "Why doesn't someone ask me what I'd like to do?"
18) "I don't care what happens to her; it's not my life."
19) "No one will miss me if I don't go."
20) "You always let Pat go. Why can't I?"

Most families struggle with communication. Here's what one family did when communication shut down between the parents and their son.

Jean and Karl worried about fourteen-year-old Kevin. About six months earlier he suddenly had become secretive, hiding behind his closed bedroom door, avoiding all contact with the family. Determined to keep Kevin in touch with the family even if he was a teenager, Jean and Karl made Kevin join them and their other two children for a day at a local amusement park. At first Kevin moped around, but within an hour of arriving at the park, he was laughing and screaming and acting like the old Kevin. That night after a full day of fun, Kevin's parents knocked on his bedroom door to thank him for going with them. During the conversation Karl asked, "Is something wrong? Your mom and I have worried about you for several months, but today proves you still want to be a part of our family. We love you. How can we help?"

Quickly Kevin told them his problems. Several older kids at school had offered Kevin marijuana. He didn't know what to do, so he'd been smoking it with them after school. He felt trapped—and guilty. The only way he knew to handle it was to withdraw. Fortunately, Jean and Karl didn't blow up. Instead they sat and calmly talked with Kevin about the problem and his options. Soon they had several ideas Kevin could use.

Later, Karl told me how devastating the news was, but he was determined to help Kevin remain part of the family. His efforts paid off in open communication before it was too late.

TODAY'S CHALLENGE

Listen to the statements your teenager makes today. Do any of these indicate a need you think your teenager is missing? What will you do about it?

TODAY'S REFLECTIONS

» This study reminds me ...
» A thought God has brought to mind ...
» I want to focus on ...

TODAY'S PRAYER

» Pray that your words today will be "like apples of gold in settings of silver"—valuable to those who hear them.

77

IDENTIFY THE WOUNDS: HURT CAUSED BY TEENAGERS

God Speaks . . .
Psalm 25:7

Following a recent speaking engagement, I walked out to the church parking lot with the associate pastor and his wife. He asked me to remember their eighteen-year-old son in prayer. Their son currently lived at home while waiting for a trial date to determine the severity of his punishment for making and selling illegal drugs. Since this was his second arrest, the young man faced three to five years in prison.

The pastor explained how his previous church had asked him to resign because of his son's problems. These hurting parents felt an enormous amount of humiliation and embarrassment, as well as rejection from those they had considered their closest friends. Even though they had sought help from a professional counselor, the hurt remained. Fortunately, the church where they currently served was supportive and encouraging to this grieving family.

The pastor asked me to talk with his son, so I took the young man out to get an ice cream cone. Knowing I couldn't change the circumstances, I reassured the teenager that his parents loved him very much and only wanted the best for him. As we talked, the young man shared how he was coping with the embarrassment and pain in his own life. He expressed great sorrow that he had hurt his family. I challenged him to reconcile with his family, especially his parents. He assured me he would.

Early Tuesday morning, as the pastor drove me to the airport, he shared how their family had stayed up until 2 *a.m.* working through numerous issues that had damaged family relationships. He explained that even though his son would have to suffer the consequences of his crime, he felt the family had experienced forgiveness and peace.

While effective communication can create and restore some parent–teen relationships, for many families this is not enough. Their wounds are too deep. Their hurt is too intense. For them the pain continues no matter what they say or do. To meet the needs of their teenagers, these families must deal with past wounds, identify the problems that caused the pain, grieve for the broken relationships, and move toward forgiveness. Easily said—tough to do!

The first step in healing the hurts is to identify the wounds. In this devotion, let's look at the wounds caused by your teenager. The list of damaging behaviors that teenagers get into can be extensive and still not include the action or behavior that paralyzes your family. It is necessary, however, to identify the situation that causes the hurt before healing can begin. From the list below select the behavior(s) you feel caused the hurt that needs healing in your family. Write in other behaviors that relate to your family's current emotional status.

- ❒ use of drugs and/or alcohol
- ❒ school dropout
- ❒ uncontrolled rage
- ❒ trouble with the law
- ❒ smoking
- ❒ self-mutilation
- ❒ attempted suicide
- ❒ runaway
- ❒ sexual activity
- ❒ eating disorders
- ❒ pregnancy
- ❒ verbal abuse
- ❒ pornography
- ❒ reckless driving
- ❒ homosexuality
- ❒ other

Although some activities happened in the past, they still can control family relationships. The psalmist has a word to encourage parents. God is a God of forgiveness. He has forgiven you, so you can forgive others.

TODAY'S CHALLENGE

Write the behavior of your teenager that has most damaged the family. Crumble up the paper and throw it away. Reflect on what it will take to rid your family of that behavior (not the teenager, but the behavior).

TODAY'S REFLECTIONS

» This study reminds me ...
» A thought God has brought to mind ...
» I want to focus on ...

TODAY'S PRAYER

» Pray that God will begin the healing in you, starting today.

NOTES

_____
_____
_____
_____
_____
_____

78
IDENTIFY THE WOUNDS: HURT CAUSED BY PARENTS

God Speaks . . .
1 Peter 4:3-7

Teenagers are not the only ones who create hard-to-heal wounds. Parents bear responsibility too. In several of the situations identified below, you may feel more like the victim and less like the one who caused the pain. Yet it is important to understand how these situations and behaviors hold family relationships hostage. Admitting the problem is the first vital step to healing.

Has your family been hurt by a damaged marriage?

❑ marital conflict, but still living together
❑ marital conflict resulting in separation
❑ marital conflict resulting in divorce
❑ remarriage with no other children involved except the teenager
❑ remarriage with other children involved

The Stepfamily Foundation helps families learn to live in stepfamily situations. Their statistics about stepfamilies look like this:

- Sixty percent of second marriages end in divorce, according to the U.S. Census Bureau.

- Fifty percent of the children in the U.S. live in a family that will experience divorce before the child turns 18.
- The prediction is that more Americans will live in stepfamilies than in nuclear families by the year 2000.[23]

Has your family been damaged by some form of abuse?

❏ physical abuse   ❏ emotional abuse   ❏ sexual abuse

According to Josh McDowell, physical abuse includes "all acts that create injury or a substantial and unnecessary risk of injury. Violent shaking or slapping, shoving, kicking, and punching are all forms of physical abuse."[24] Emotional abuse is more difficult to determine because it involves verbal attacks, blaming, or belittling, but also may include an attitude of disrespect for the teenager. Other than related medical problems such as bruises or burns, the abused teenager may feel guilt, a lack of trust, aggression, poor social skills, emotional withdrawal, or a desire to run away.

Sexual abuse involves any kind of sexual contact, observation, or conversation between someone else and a child, with the exploiter receiving sexual gratification from the experience. The exploiter can be someone in the family (including another child) or someone outside the family.[25]

Has your family been damaged by other situations?

❏ rage or uncontrolled anger
❏ neglect (defined as a parent's failure to take care of the child's basic needs and well-being in an adequate way)
❏ long-term illness
❏ change in job (fired, "phased out," or demoted; new location involving a move; promotion involving more time away from family)
❏ death of family member that you are still grieving
❏ substance abuse (alcohol and/or drugs)
❏ other_____

What event has created the greatest hurt in your family?

What do you think must happen for this hurt to heal?

TODAY'S CHALLENGE

As you think about past negative experiences in your family, also focus on one or two experiences that were fun for everyone.

TODAY'S REFLECTIONS

- » This study reminds me …
- » A thought God has brought to mind …
- » I want to focus on …

TODAY'S PRAYER

- » Pray for forgiveness from God for your actions that may have damaged your family's relationships.

NOTES

_____
_____
_____
_____
_____

79
GRIEF, GUILT, AND OTHER FEELINGS

God Speaks...
Ephesians 1:7

Emotions and feelings can prevent the hurt from healing. Have you or other family members experienced the following?

- Pride: "What will other people think?"
- Guilt: "Where did I go wrong?"
- Anger: "How could he do that to me?"
- Shame: "I can never show my face in public again."
- Loneliness: "I can't talk to anyone; it's just too personal."
- Fear: "Will we ever be a normal family again?"
- Grief: "I've lost the most precious part of me."
- Bitterness: "She always does something to make me feel lousy."

One of the strongest emotions associated with a past hurt is guilt. Whether you did the wounding or you were the one wounded by another's behavior, guilt can occur. If, for example, you and your spouse divorced, perhaps you feel guilty for the damage done to your children. If your teenager is participating in a dangerous activity that you know is wrong, you may feel guilty for not meeting that teenager's need. Actually the pain of guilt can be a warning that protects relationships. For example, if a person feels guilty for a certain behavior, the guilt may stop the person from continuing that behavior. Bruce Hamstra, in *Why Good People Do Bad Things,* explains the difference between good guilt and bad guilt:

- Good guilt serves as a compass for your personal standards.
- Good guilt helps you to control destructive, hurtful impulses.
- Good guilt allows you to experience the pain of your mistakes and take corrective actions.
- Good guilt, if honestly acknowledged, can lead to personal growth, the making of amends, and perhaps even forgiveness.
- Guilt is not helpful when it stems from things that are truly not your fault.
- Guilt is not helpful when you have unintentionally hurt or neglected someone, although apologies may be in order.
- Guilt is not helpful when it's unfairly used by others to manipulate you or impede your personal growth.
- Guilt is not helpful when the hurtful acts were not foreseeable or preventable.
- Guilt is not helpful when your thoughts, feelings, or actions didn't actually hurt anyone else.[26]

Look over Hamstra's list. Circle the type of guilt you feel. Figure out what kind of guilt you have and what has caused the feeling.

In earlier devotions you saw the importance of grieving the loss of unmet needs in your life. Grieving the hurt in family relationships brings healing too. You may have shed many tears over the painful situation that has wounded your family. It may not be necessary to cry again, but it is necessary to realize that in some way the family has been hurt, or damaged, or experienced a broken relationship. In divorce the grief is often not recognized because of the feelings of failure. But divorce is the death of a relationship that deserves to be grieved. You may have to grieve the fact that your teenager is not living up to your hopes and expectations. You may have to grieve that your teenager has made poor choices and must suffer the consequences. You may have to grieve that you have hurt others with your poor choices. For some people grief is a private matter. For others it helps to grieve and receive comfort. Don't bypass this important step in healing.

For what do you need to grieve?

With whom can you share this grief?

TODAY'S CHALLENGE

Write today's verse on an index card to carry with you. As you think about grief and guilt, read these words of assurance.

TODAY'S REFLECTIONS

» This study reminds me . . .
» A thought God has brought to mind . . .
» I want to focus on . . .

TODAY'S PRAYER

» Pray for God's grace in facing a hurtful situation and learning from it.

NOTES

_____
_____
_____
_____

80
FIND REPENTANCE AND FORGIVENESS

God Speaks . . .
Jeremiah 15:19

Healing the deepest hurts takes time and effort. The process stirs up painful memories and creates heart-wrenching emotions. Are you content to live with the guilt and pain in your family, or do you want to move on? To deal with the wounding, you can either blame others, society, your teenager, the circumstances, even God, or you can seek forgiveness. If you are the one who has been wounded, then you can do the forgiving. If you are the one who has created the hurtful situation, then you must ask for forgiveness.

Bruce Hamstra, in *Why Good People Do Bad Things*, explains the great value of forgiveness: "Forgiveness is a powerful equalizer: It helps free the victim of the bitterness and anger that eats away at the spirit while at the same time liberating the perpetrator from much of his or her guilt. It allows all involved a better chance to get on with their lives."[27]

Today you'll look at the process to use in being forgiven. If your actions or attitudes have hurt your family, your asking for forgiveness starts with repentance. Repentance is more than saying, "I'm sorry."

This shallow approach is dispensed too often without sincerity. A sincere request for forgiveness might sound like this:

"I was wrong. I made mistakes that hurt you. I regret my part in hurting you. I want to change the feelings between us."

Repentance involves both a change of mind (a new attitude) and a change of direction (a different action). We are most familiar with repenting and asking God for His forgiveness. Communicating with God is the place to start as you work to restore a relationship within your family. Be direct in identifying the hurtful action. State your repentance, asking God to begin the healing. Next, go to those in your family, including your teenager, who have been affected by your wounding action or attitude. Confess your hurtful action or attitude honestly. Ask for the other person's forgiveness. You might say something like the statement above or this:

"I'm trying to rebuild our relationship. I am hurting because I have hurt you. I want things to be better between us. Please forgive me for my hurtful action. I can make excuses, but they don't really matter. I just want things to be better between us."

Is an apology enough? I don't think so. Here's the hard part. You must *live your repentance* before the other person. Show your changed attitude in the way you relate to your teenager. Show consideration and a caring concern for your teenager. Don't repeat the offending behavior. Draw strength from knowing God has already forgiven you.

Thinking about your own situation, ask God's forgiveness. Write an apology to your teenager and other family members, if they were involved:_____

_____

_____

List several ways you can live your repentance before your family:

_____

_____

TODAY'S CHALLENGE

How does the promise in Jeremiah 15:19 encourage you to seek repentance and healing?

TODAY'S REFLECTIONS

- » This study reminds me ...
- » A thought God has brought to mind ...
- » I want to focus on ...

TODAY'S PRAYER

- » Pray for a change of heart and direction as you handle a hurt in your family. Pray for God's great wisdom working through you.
- » Thank God for the many times He has forgiven you.

NOTES

81
FORGIVE AND BE FREE

God Speaks...
Psalm 139:23-24

Yesterday you looked at forgiving the hurt from the point of view of the person who needed to repent and be forgiven. Today consider how to find forgiveness when you and your family have been wounded by your teenager's behavior. In today's study you will learn how to offer forgiveness. David Augsburger, in *The Freedom of Forgiveness*, suggests a four-step process of forgiveness that I've adapted for parents.

1) *Forgive immediately* before bitterness, guilt, or hurt get into your thoughts and turn into vindictive revenge. Augsburger suggests the way to handle bitterness once it has taken hold is to "stop thinking about yourself. Don't tolerate those thoughts of self-pity. Don't permit those angry thoughts of self-defensiveness to master you."[28] To heal you must stop the cycle of hurt and get on with life.

2) *Forgive continually* so that you are focused on others, rather than yourself. This lifestyle accepts others as they are. This is not a shallow tolerance of others or letting others manipulate your feelings. Forgiveness does not condone the action. It does not depend on any change in the offender's behavior. There are no guarantees that the offensive behavior won't happen again. Continual forgiveness, however, realizes that life is

too valuable to spend in anger, self-pity, or revenge. You will only have this teenager in your home for a few short years, then the teenager goes into the world. Even in close families, children form lives of their own, and parents learn to live in "an empty nest." Forgive so these last few years together can be more pleasant and acceptable, rather than bitter, sad, difficult days.

3) *Forgive and forget.* It may not be possible to completely remove the hurt from your memory or the consequences of the hurt from reality. It is possible, however, to stop rehashing the problem with "if onlys" and "what ifs." When you forgive and forget, the situation no longer has power over you. You have chosen to let those old feelings go. Forgiving and forgetting protect the forgiver from bitterness and hate, and offer, instead, peace of mind.

4) *Forgive and be healed.* Forgiveness is an active word. You can express your forgiveness before the teenager asks for forgiveness. You might say, "I forgive you for hurting me by your habitual drinking. I don't like your behavior, and I'm going to help you stop. But I love you, and I'm not going to let this come between us."

This kind of forgiveness brings healing because it is "acceptance with no exception. It accepts not only the hurt you've received, it accepts the one who did the hurting, and it accepts the loss caused by the hurtful actions or words. It makes no exceptions," according to Augsburger.[29] You can forgive, forget, and be healed because Christ did it for you.

- Who do you need to forgive?
- How will you state your forgiveness?
- How do you think your forgiveness can bring healing to such a painful situation?
- What keeps you from forgiving?

TODAY'S CHALLENGE

What sounds good in theory can be tough in reality. Begin the forgiving process today by forgiving small actions that normally irritate you.

TODAY'S REFLECTIONS

- » This study reminds me ...
- » A thought God has brought to mind ...
- » I want to focus on ...

TODAY'S PRAYER

- » Pray Psalm 139:23-24.

NOTES

82
WHEN TO ASK FOR HELP

God Speaks . . .
Matthew 9:12

Healing deep hurts within a family may require more than a few honest discussions between you and your teenager. There are times when you may need to seek outside help in the healing process. If you continue to reap the consequences of an action that occurred long ago, your emotions may be too embedded to push aside. If you are dealing with the consequences of an action that took place recently, your emotions may be too raw to handle with the person involved. If the action that causes the hurt continues, you will have a hard time healing.

Asking for professional help is not a sign of weakness, but of strength. Acknowledging the need for another's help says, "I am doing the best job I can, but God has not gifted me in understanding all I need to know in order to help my teenager (or in order to help myself). I need help from someone else." A professional counselor can determine the extent to which your teenager needs professional help, and more importantly, can give both you and your teenager perspective on the situation. Before seeking professional help, use these questions suggested by psychotherapist and psychologist Les Parrott III, to determine whether to involve a counselor or not. Remember also that you need to be concerned about a pattern of behavior, not necessarily a single incident.[30]

- Is your teenager quiet for long periods of time or withdrawn from friends and regular activities?
- Is your teenager close to dropping out of or failing school?
- Is your teenager obsessed with food, diets, and exercise?
- Is your teenager involved in any form of self-mutilation (cuts, burns, teeth marks)?
- Does your teenager fear being left alone with a member of your family, a neighbor, or some other person? Is there any chance sexual abuse has occurred or is taking place now?
- Is your teenager depressed?
- Is your teenager interested in the occult or black magic?
- Is your teenager involved in several situations of vandalism or fights?
- Is your teenager sexually active?
- Is your teenager hearing voices, hallucinating, or out of touch with reality?
- Is your teenager having morbid thoughts or talking about death?
- Is your teenager having trouble sleeping, eating, staying focused on a task, or any other radical change in behavior?
- Is your teenager drinking, driving and drinking, using drugs, or huffing paint, glue, or other substances?
- Is your teenager experiencing panic attacks with intense periods of anxiety?

To locate professional help, ask for referrals from your family physician, a minister, a school counselor, or friends who also have teenagers. A preliminary phone call to the professional will give you information about that person's areas of specialization and expectations. If you want someone with a Christian frame of reference, ask that question when you first talk with the professional.

If you can't afford professional counseling (although many insurance carriers cover professional counseling), another possibility is to join a support group for either you or your teenager. Look in the "Yellow Pages" of your phone directory or in your local newspaper for groups, times, and meeting places. You will find support groups designed for specific problems such as Al-Anon for children of alcoholics, support groups associated with treatment hospitals, and support groups sponsored by local churches.

TODAY'S CHALLENGE

Consider how a Christian support group could help you with your problem.

TODAY'S REFLECTIONS

» This study reminds me …
» A thought God has brought to mind …
» I want to focus on …

TODAY'S PRAYER

» Thank God for being the Great Physician whose healing powers work through dedicated professionals.

NOTES

_____
_____
_____
_____

83
WHEN THE HURTING STOPS

God Speaks . . .
Proverbs 24:14
Romans 11:11

Once forgiveness is offered, healing can begin. You may not feel like everything is back to normal (whatever that is when living with a teenager!), but you should see improvement in your relationship with your teenager. And you should be able to implement the process of meeting needs more effectively. Let the following ideas get you back on track.

1) *Don't live under the circumstances.* You control your thoughts and feelings. Don't be a victim. Don't let others continue to wound you. Take charge of the circumstances.

2) *Learn from the past.* Model how to accept responsibility for your actions. Stop blaming yourself or others. Be the best parent you can be—not perfect—just the best.

3) *Remember that failure is never final.* Mistakes, whether yours or your teenager's, can be overcome. View problems as challenges and opportunities rather than further failures.

4) *Look for influences that undermine the healing process.* Listen to what your teenager says. Is the teenager being taunted by peers? Are health problems creating painful thoughts? Is a teenager's busy schedule overwhelming?

5) *Let others give you perspective.* This could be an adult friend, a youth minister, a counselor, a professional for you or your teenager.

6) *Delete negative talk and thoughts from your vocabulary.* This is not a matter of "can't" but of "will." You control your negative feelings and actions.

7) *Focus on the future.* What do you want for your teenager? What do you want for your family? Build on the strengths you see in your family. Recognize that there is always room to grow.

8) *Love your teenager, no matter what.* Ken Chafin puts it this way: "There are few needs as strong when trouble comes as the need for the love and acceptance of parents. Because this is true it means that there is no place where there is greater potential for healing than in a family which loves and cares."[31]

TODAY'S CHALLENGE

You and your teenager cannot fall beyond God's recovery. Which idea today will help you the most?

TODAY'S REFLECTIONS

» This study reminds me ...
» A thought God has brought to mind ...
» I want to focus on ...

TODAY'S PRAYER

» Thank God for "wisdom [that] is sweet to your soul" and for the hope it brings.

84
RELATIONSHIP GOALS

God Speaks . . .
Psalm 143:8

At one time Howard Hill was considered one of the greatest archers who ever lived. He repeatedly hit a target dead center. After the first arrow struck the bull's eye, he then split that arrow with his next shot. I believe you as a parent could outshoot Howard Hill on his best day—even if you had never picked up a bow and arrow in your life. Here's how: Blindfold Hill and spin him around a couple of times until he doesn't know where the target is, then I guarantee that you will have a better chance at hitting the target more consistently than Howard Hill. Maybe you're wondering, "How in the world do you expect a guy to hit a target he can't see?" That's a good question. Here's a better one: If Howard Hill couldn't hit a target he couldn't see, how do you expect to hit a target you don't have? Zig Ziglar says, "It's just as difficult to reach a destination you don't have as it is to come back from a place you've never been."[32] What is your target in your relationship with your teenager?

That's what these next few devotions are designed to do. They will help you define and set specific goals to assist you in improving and strengthening your relationship with your teenager. As a parent your overall goal is to help move your teenager from a parent-dependent child to a self-controlled, independent adult. The specifics for accomplishing that huge task can be found in setting small, achievable, intermediate goals along the way.

Consider why it's important to set goals.

- The psalmist knew the value of having a direction and purpose. Without goals we become stagnant, repeating behavior that may leave us feeling frustrated, bored, or hopeless.
- Goals encourage us to look forward to new experiences and challenges. Setting a goal forces us to stretch physically, emotionally, mental, socially, or spiritually.
- Goals guide the way we establish priorities in our lives. For example, if the goal is to pay more attention to your teenager, you may have to give up working late every night or serving on several committees at church in order to have time to spend with your teenager.
- Goals determine the way we make decisions. If your goal is to give more attention to your teenager, then that goal helps you decide about a job transfer that involves more traveling.
- Goals offer security because you know where you are going. Goals provide the motivation to get there. The goal of paying more attention to your teenager motivates you to get your work done at the office so you won't have to bring it home.
- Finally, goals are a hedge against settling for mediocrity. With a goal you hold out for a higher pattern of behavior, rather than settling for the same behavior that may be more negative and selfish.

TODAY'S CHALLENGE

Write down a few goals you have set for yourself in the past. What did you do to achieve those goals? How successful were you in reaching your goals?

TODAY'S REFLECTIONS

» This study reminds me ...
» A thought God has brought to mind ...
» I want to focus on ...

TODAY'S PRAYER

» Pray that God will show you the way to go as you evaluate how to help your teenager.

NOTES

_____
_____
_____
_____
_____
_____
_____
_____
_____
_____
_____
_____

85
RELATIONSHIP GOAL SETTING

God Speaks . . .

Proverbs 14:22

Philippians 4:13

To set an effective goal, you must include these basic parts.

Part I — A Specific, Clear, Measurable Purpose

A goal should be specific enough to be written down, clear enough to be remembered, and measurable enough to be accomplished. A parent might choose the goal of "making my teenager a better person," but how do you know when "better" is achieved? A measurable goal has a specific outcome that can be examined, understood, or accomplished. A more focused goal might be "to help my teenager deal with her anger by giving her several coping options." Another goal might be "to support my teenager in his struggle with relationships with his friends by frequently praising his strong qualities."

Set your goal high enough to challenge you and your teenager to grow. Be careful not to set your goal so high, however, that you get discouraged when you never see success.

Part 2—A Plan with Specific Steps

A goal should have a plan that helps you reach the goal. This plan may involve one step or several steps, depending on the complexity of the goal. For example, for the goal "to help my teenager deal with her anger by giving her several coping options," a parent might list two or three steps like these:

- Step 1—Discuss how destructive anger looks by evaluating stories in the news.
- Step 2—Talk about ways to cope with anger (shooting baskets, writing a letter to the person who is the source of the teenager's anger—but not sending it, talking about the situation to a good listener, confronting the person who angered you).
- Step 3—Model how to handle a frustrating situation without getting angry.

A plan like this breaks down the goal into manageable portions so you don't feel overwhelmed. If one step fails to work, move to the next step.

Part 3—A Time for Completion

A goal should have a time limit that keeps you moving forward, rather than procrastinating. The time limit also helps you identify whether a goal is long-term, involving several months to several years, or short-term, that can be achieved in a day, a week, or a month. For example, a long-term goal might be to get your high school dropout back on track academically. Interim victories move you toward your ultimate goal. Set dates for short-term goals to be accomplished too. Celebrate the achievement of short-term goals, as well as longer goals. If you don't achieve your goal in the designated time, evaluate your goal, look at your plans to reach the goal, and set another date.

There are several different kinds of goals. Here are two that relate to teenagers.

- Fantasy goals are fun, but not achievable by most of us. These may include playing in a professional sport, living in the tropics, creating the world's greatest invention, writing a top-ten bestseller, starring on Broadway, feeding the starving—well, you get the picture. Encourage and support your teenager's goals, fantasies or not. Many people have successfully accomplished their fantasy goals because a parent encouraged their dreams.
- Goals that are never discussed or defined may disappear, not for lack of vision, but because the person never worked through how to make the goal a reality. These missed goals may include such basic areas as getting a college education, owning a home, or starting a business you're interested in.

TODAY'S CHALLENGE

Ask different people what their goals were in the past. Listen to how they achieved these goals.

TODAY'S REFLECTIONS

- » This study reminds me ...
- » A thought God has brought to mind ...
- » I want to focus on ...

TODAY'S PRAYER

- » Pray that God will strengthen you as you work on the process of setting goals for you and your teenager.
- » Ask God to help you be faithful to the plans you make.

86
MAKING YOUR GOALS A REALITY

God Speaks . . .
1 Timothy 1:5

Paul wrote this letter to Timothy to warn his people away from false doctrines. Paul issued this warning because he loved Timothy and the people under Timothy's leadership. Love is an excellent goal to set in any intimate, revolutionary relationship.

Today's devotion is designed to give you goal-setting opportunities. Determine what you want to accomplish in the different areas of relationships. If you have started working toward a goal, record it here. Mark progress by using the margins to identify interim victories and short-term accomplishments. Under each category, I have suggested an example to start you thinking.

1) My Personal Relationship Goals
   (An example)
   - Goal: Explain to my wife why I have so much trouble showing affection to our teenagers.
   - Plan: Share the ideas concerning how the past influences our needs as discussed in these devotions.
   - Accomplish by (time): over the weekend.

(Your own goal)
- Goal:
- Plan:
- Accomplish by (time):

2) Goals Involving Family (spouse, other children, other significant adults, extended family)

   (An example)
   - Goal: Strengthen a relationship with my oldest child, who lives away from home.
   - Plan: Take her to dinner and ask her to share what she wishes I had done for her during her teen years; ask for forgiveness for times when I didn't meet my child's needs; state a desire to strengthen our relationship; ask for ideas on how to do this.
   - Accomplish by (time): midsummer.

   (Your own goal)
   - Goal:
   - Plan:
   - Accomplish by (time):

3) Goals Involving My Teenager

   (An example)
   - Goal: Understand my teenager's world by getting involved in that world.
   - Plan: Ask teenager about sports schedule of school team; urge teenager to bring friends over one weekend.
   - Accomplish by (time): two weeks.

   (Your own goal)
   - Goal:
   - Plan:

- Accomplish by (time):

TODAY'S CHALLENGE

Set a goal that can be accomplished today; then carry it out.

TODAY'S REFLECTIONS

» This study reminds me …
» A thought God has brought to mind …
» I want to focus on …

TODAY'S PRAYER

» Pray for "a pure heart and a good conscience and a sincere faith" as you set these goals.
» Ask God to help you succeed in one goal as a way of encouraging you to continue to change the way you relate to your teenager.

NOTES

87
HANGING ON TO HOPE

God Speaks . . .
Hebrews 6:19

Part of the goal-setting process involves helping teenagers set personal goals to develop their independence. This presents a dilemma in knowing how much responsibility to give your teenager so that growth toward independence doesn't happen too early or too late. A teenager faced with tough decisions too early may not be prepared to handle the consequences of a poor decision. A teenager given too many decisions where he continually fails may have a hard time learning to take responsibility. On the other hand, if a parent maintains total control, that teenager doesn't learn how to make decisions or accept responsibility. When this teenager leaves home without having participated in significant decision making, he may make unhealthy decisions that jeopardize his future, his health, relationships, and other areas of life.

A few teenagers, who never get a chance to make their own decisions, never grow up, and fail to leave home. Since goals tie into decision making, think through these areas using the revolutionary insights you've learned.

- Areas where I am willing to let my teenager make decisions:

- Areas where I am not ready to let my teenager made decisions:

Show these two lists to your teenager. Talk about the decision-making process. Discuss goals that will allow your teenager to take over more decision making in his life.

Mall security called Marie Citron to say that her son Maddox was being held for shoplifting. With Maddox only thirteen years old, Marie could see a life of crime unfolding before her. The store agreed not to prosecute if Maddox would work for two weekends straightening up their storage room under the supervision of his mother. Everyone agreed to the punishment.

When they got home, Marie Citron sat Maddox down and talked with him about shoplifting. Recognizing a cry for attention, she asked Maddox questions about what he had expected to happen and what he wanted to see happen. After several hours of talking, Maddox and his mother set a goal to meet Maddox's need for some focused attention from his single-parent mom. Maddox and Marie decided to spend one Saturday morning a month doing something Maddox enjoyed and one Tuesday night a month doing something Marie enjoyed. Both mother and son would work or play together for the next six months. Marie later told me that the shoplifting incident actually brought her closer to her son than she had been in years.

Using the Revolutionary Relationship ideas discussed in this book, I hope you see how to teach your teenager to be an independent individual while improving the relationship between the two of you. Most parents love their teenagers and want their teenagers to make it through the adolescent years with as few scars as possible. Teenagers face tremendous pressures and temptations to participate in the alternate values of the culture around them. I want you to see that there is hope. God assures us of that hope.

TODAY'S CHALLENGE

Write this verse with its message of hope in a place where you will see it frequently today.

TODAY'S REFLECTIONS

- » This study reminds me ...
- » A thought God has brought to mind ...
- » I want to focus on ...

TODAY'S PRAYER

- » Thank God for His "anchor" of hope.
- » Ask God to make hope real to other family members too.

NOTES

_____
_____
_____
_____
_____

88
TOP TEN THINGS PARENTS WOULD LIKE TO HEAR FROM THEIR TEENAGERS

God Speaks . . .
Jeremiah 33:3

A popular late-night TV host has made the listing of ten items a celebrated way of dispensing humorous information. Here's my list of "Top Ten Things Parents Would Like to Hear from Their Teenager (but won't until the teenager develops into a mature adult!)":

10) "Thanks, folks, for giving me rules to live by."

9) "Of course, that's a fair and reasonable punishment."

8) "I've decided not to go out tonight because I want to spend time at home with the family."

7) "I'm tired of pizza and hamburgers. Why don't we have a veggie plate for dinner?"

6) "I'd be delighted to clean up my room and the bathroom."

5) "I realize I don't know everything. I need your advice."

4) "I filled up the car with gas, and checked the tires and oil for you."

3) "I don't really need a car, the latest brand-name clothing, or the hottest CD."

2) "How was your day?"

1) "Can I take out the garbage for you?"

Maybe you won't hear these anytime soon, but I believe after you've implemented several of the ideas in these devotions, you might hear something like this—"I love you, Mom." "I love you, Dad." "Thanks for being here for me." "I'm proud to be your son." "I'm glad I'm your daughter."

Many parents feel so hopeless and embattled in their relationships with their teenagers that they would settle for any small semblance of peace and agreement. I hope you've seen, however, that if we make a genuine effort to understand one another, we can experience healing, forgiveness, and grace. In time, the home environment can become a place of love and laughter as you delight in your teenager. Teenagers and parents are really not as far apart as they think they are.

TODAY'S CHALLENGE

Decide today what would be the most surprising statement to come from your teenager.

TODAY'S REFLECTIONS

» This study reminds me ...
» A thought God has brought to mind ...
» I want to focus on ...

TODAY'S PRAYER

» Pray a prayer of thanksgiving in response to today's Scripture.

89
KEEPING THE RELATIONSHIP REVOLUTION ALIVE

God Speaks...
Psalm 37:4

Philippians 4:6-7

Keeping the Relationship Revolution alive begins with consistency and commitment. Here are five ideas to help you continue to experience a positive, enjoyable time with your teenager as you meet his or her needs.

1) Post the NEEDS acrostic where every family member can see it—the refrigerator, by the phone, on a bathroom mirror, beside the door everyone uses to leave the house.

2) Talk about meeting the different needs in conversations with your family. Pick a need and let it be the topic of conversation during an evening meal. Pick a need and let every family member write out how he or she would like to have that need met in their life.

3) Get in the habit of talking to your teenager every day. Visiting late at night is ideal, or while playing basketball, taking a walk after supper, or driving your teenager to an event. The conversations don't have to be deep, just regular.

4) Set aside one day a month for each child. If a full day is not possible, try half-days. Don't let anything interfere with this time.

"As a single mom with three teenage girls, I felt like a prisoner in my own home," Toni Reames laughed. "Fights, slammed doors, raised voices, name-calling, and that dreaded silent treatment dominated our existence together. Then I heard Rodney speak at our church. I suddenly realized I was so stressed out about meeting the physical needs of my girls that I'd forgotten about all the other needs. The next day I sat my girls down, apologized for not helping them through these tough teen years, and promised to do better. The girls were so surprised they didn't say anything at the time. Later, however, each reassured me privately that I wasn't doing that bad a job. But I realized I needed to spend time with each girl individually. So once a month I'm trying the 'do-what-the-teenager-wants-to-do' thing, and it's been fun. Everybody's been a little more pleasant most of the time. I may survive their teenage years after all!"

5) Once a month, assess the strength of your relations with your teenager and others in the family. Look for any negative changes in behavior that might warn of an unmet need. Reflect on how your needs are being met. Rejoice with God that He is still in charge.

TODAY'S CHALLENGE

Make a list of the anxieties you still have about parenting your teenager. Read Philippians 4:6-7 several times.

TODAY'S REFLECTIONS

» This study reminds me …
» A thought God has brought to mind …
» I want to focus on …

TODAY'S PRAYER

» Pray for God to be so real to you that you feel encouragement and delight in His presence.

NOTES

90
THE BEST NEWS A PARENT CAN HEAR

God Speaks...
Jude 24-25

Twenty-year-old Kory Herring shared this with me not too long ago. "According to the statistics, I'm supposed to be a drugged-out alcoholic whose favorite pastimes are sexual intercourse and drunken driving. I'm surprised I even have time to fight with my parents and my siblings. Last year in high school 40 percent of me was supposed to fear the violence in my school, a good reason to drop out of school. Right? I'm supposed to carry a beeper, prefer permanent tattoos to body piercing, and take lessons in how to shoot a gun instead of how to play a musical instrument. Over the years I presumably have increased my use of the seatbelt in my car and wear a crash helmet when riding my motorbike, but I've also increased my use of cigarettes and cocaine. And, because I'm expected to speed and drive drunk, I'm supposed to die in either an automobile accident, as a homicide, or a suicide.

"Well, I'm telling you that's not going to happen. I actually made it through my teen years without becoming a smoking, drugged-out, sexually active alcoholic. While I saw problems in my school, that didn't stop me from learning the Pythagorean theorem or how to speak proper English in the real world. During my teen years I ran track for my high school, stayed active in youth group at church, and dated only occasionally (because it was so expensive!). I've never run away from home, although I offered to help my brother run away after he tore up my stereo (but that's another story). I've never hit my dad or thrown anything at my mother. And now that I live in a college dorm, I actually miss having someone "remind" me to put the dirty clothes in the hamper. (Do you know how bad sweaty, dirty clothes can make a room smell?)

"I called my mom yesterday to assure her that I was surviving college. But my real reason was to thank her and Dad for being the kind of parents I needed when I was a teenager. Oh, sure, they used me for slave labor to do regular chores around the house—like the dreaded take-out-the-garbage task and the help-your-dad-with-the-yard requirement. They insisted I come in before 1 *a.m.* and go to school every day, even when I didn't have a required research paper completed. They gave advice when I needed it, and somehow knew when not to share advice when I didn't want it. They refused to let me watch MTV all day and actually locked me out of pornographic sites on the Internet. They followed me to all my track meets, chauffeured me to all kinds of events, listened to my frustrations when I lost the Student Body office, and cared about me no matter what my grades were. I just wanted to thank Mom for all the peanut butter and jelly sandwiches and brownies she made for lunches so I wouldn't have to eat school food, and all the ice cream late at night when I needed to talk. They loved me no matter what I did. I may not be the typical teenager—well, not anymore 'cause I just turned twenty—but I do know there are lots of almost normal young people out there just like me with really neat parents. I think we're all going to be OK."

TODAY'S CHALLENGE

Reflect on what your assessment of yourself would have been at twenty. Then look into the future and decide what you think your teenager will say about himself at twenty.

TODAY'S REFLECTIONS

- » This study reminds me …
- » A thought God has brought to mind …
- » I want to focus on …

TODAY'S PRAYER

- » Pray Jude 24-25 as not only a closing benediction, but as a renewal of God's presence in your life.

NOTES

_____
_____
_____
_____
_____
_____

ENDNOTES

1. Studies cited in "Family and School Support Matter," Assets, Search Institute (Winter 1997), 12, and "Factors that Affect Children's Use of Drugs," Family Research Council: In Focus, 1998, www.frc.org/frc/infocus/ef9864dr.html.
2. Reported in "Family School Aids Skills," Assets, Search Institute (Autumn 1996), 12.
3. Cited in "Connections to Parents Matter," Assets, Search Institute (Summer 1997), 11.
4. Gallup Youth Survey, Emerging Trends (September 1997). (Internet)
5. Mary Pipher, Reviving Ophelia: Saving the Selves of Adolescent Girls (New York: Ballentine, 1994), 83.
6. Ibid, 60.
7. Daniel Goleman, Emotional Intelligence (New York: Bantam, 1995), 91-92.
8. Walt Mueller, "Rediscovering Love," Living with Teenagers (February 1998), 9.
9. Ross Campbell, How to Reallg Love Your Teenager (Wheaton, Il.: Victor, 1981), 29-30.
10. Robert L. Maginnis, "Family and Parenting Matter," a speech delivered at the San Diego County's Third Substance Abuse Summit, December 12, 1997, from the Internet at www.frc.org/frc/podium/pd98alfs.html.
11. Walt Mueller, Understanding Today's Youth Culture (Wheaton: Tyndale House, 1994), 41.
12. Les Christie, "Positive Discipline," Living with Teenagers (July 1998), 14.
13. Walt Mueller, Understanding Today's Youth Culture (Wheaton: Tyndale House, 1994), 340.
14. Les Christie, "Positive Discipline," Living with Teenagers (July 1998), 16.
15. Gary and Greg Smalley, "The Secret to Raising Teenagers: A Bountiful Bank Account!" Living with Teenagers (July 1998), 26.
16. "Kids These Days: What Americans Really Think about the Next Generation," San Antonio Express-News, June 27, 1997, as quoted in "Adults Don't Approve of Kids," Youthworker, September/October 1997, 16.
17. "It's Lonely at the Tube," Youthworker Update, November 1995, 6 (Denver Post, August 22, 1995).
18. Laura Shapiro, "The Myth of Quality Time," Newsweek, May 12, 1997, 65.
19. Emerging Trends, September 1997 (Internet).

20. "Who's Who Special Report: 'What Parents of Top Teens Don't Know about Their Kids' Confirms Parents' Worst Fears," Internet at www.eci-whoswho.com/highschool/speakup/parents.html.
21. "Parents 'Out of Touch' with Teenagers' Drug Use," Youthworker, July/August 1998, 12 (USA Today, April 13, 1998).
22. Campbell Leaper, Kristin J. Anderson, and Paul Sanders, 1998: "Moderator of gender effects on parents' talk to their children: A meta-analysis," Developmental Psychology 34(l):3-27 as reported in "Moms and Dads Communicate Differently," Assets, Search Institute, Spring 1998, 14.
23. STEPFAMILY FOUNDATION website updated April 17, 1998, http://www.stepfamily.org.
24. Josh McDowell, Josh McDowell's Handbook on Counseling Youth (Waco: Word, 1996), 359.
25. Ibid., 350-51.
26. Bruce Hamstra, Why Good People Do Bad Things (New York: Carol, 1996), 37-38.
27. Ibid., 146.
28. David Aug'sburger, The Freedom of Forgiveness (Chicago: Moody, 1970), 35.
29. Ibid., 39-40.
30. Les Parrott III, Helping the Struggling Adolescent (Grand Rapids: Zondervan, 1993), 41-42.
31. Kenneth Chafin, Is There a Family in the House? (Waco: Word, Inc., 1978), 137.
32. Zig Ziglar, See You At the Top (Gretna, Louis.: Pelican, 1984), 147.

BIBLIOGRAPHY

Books

Augsburger, David. *Caring Enough to Confront.* Ventura: Regal Books, 1983._____. *The Freedom of Forgiveness.* Chicago: Moody Press, 1970.

Benson, Peter, Judy Galbraith, and Pamela Espeland. *What Kids Need to Succeed.* Minneapolis: Free Spirit Publishing, 1995.

Biehl, Bobb. *Why You Do What You Do.* Nashville: Thomas Nelson Publishers, 1993.

Campbell, Ross. *Flow to Reallg Love Your Teenager.* Wheaton, Il: Victor Books, 1981.

Chafin, Kenneth. *Is There a Family in the House?* Waco: Word, Inc., 1978. Drakeford, John W. and Claude King. *Wise Counsel.* Nashville: Life Way Press, 1993.

Faber, Adele and Elaine Mazlish. *How to Talk So Kids Will Listen and Listen So Kids Will Talk.* New York: Avon Books, 1982.

Ferguson, David. *Parenting with Intimacy Workbook.* Wheaton: Victor Books, 1995._____. *The Great Commandment Principle (Training Resource Edition).* Wheaton, Il: Tyndale, 1998.

Ferguson, David, Teresa Ferguson, and Chris and Holly Thurman. *Intimate Encounters: A Practical Guide to Discovering the Secrets of a Really Great Marriage.* Nashville: Thomas Nelson Publishers, 1994.

Gage, Rodney. *If My Parents Knew...* Nashville: Thomas Nelson Publishers, 1995. Goleman, Daniel. *Emotional Intelligence.* New York: Bantam Books, 1995.

Hamstra, Bruce. *Why Good People Do Bad Things: How to Make Moral Choices in an Immoral World.* New York: Carol Publishing Group, 1996.

Hayes, E. Kent. *Why Good Parents Have Bad Kids.* New York: Doubleday, 1989. Killinger, John R., Jr. *To Meet—To Touch—To Know: The Art of Communicating.* Nashville: The Methodist Publishing House, 1972.

Lerner, Harriet. *The Dance of Anger: A Woman's Guide to Changing the Patterns of Intimate Relationships.* New York: Harper Perennial, 1997.

McDowell, Josh. *Josh McDowell's Handbook on Counseling Youth.* Waco: Word Publishing, 1996.

Miller, Derek. *Adolescence: Psychology, Psychopathology and Psychotherapy.* New York: Jason Aronson, Inc., 1974.

Mueller, Walt. *Understanding Today's Youth Culture.* Wheaton: Tyndale House, 1994.

Parrott, Les, III. *Helping the Struggling Adolescent.* Grand Rapids: Zondervan Publishing House, 1993.

Pipher, Mary. *Reviving Ophelia: Saving the Selves of Adolescent Girls.* New York: Ballantine Books, 1994.

Wilmes, David J. *Parenting for Prevention: How to Raise a Child to Say No to Alcohol/Drugs.* Minneapolis: Johnson Institute, 1995.

Articles

"Adults Don't Approve of Kids." *Youthworker,* March/April 1998, 17.

"Connections to Parents Matter." *Assets.* Search Institute, Summer 1997, 11.

"Family and School Support Matter." *Assets.* Search Institute, Winter 1997, 12.

"Family Support Aids Social Skills." *Assets.* Search Institute, Autumn 1996, 12.

"It's Lonely at the Tube." *Youthworker Update,* November 1995, 6.

"Moms and Dads Communicate Differently." *Assets.* Search Institute, April 1998, 14.

"Parents 'Out of Touch' with Kids' Drug Use." *Youthworker,* July/August 1998, 12.

"Teenage Volunteering." *Assets.* Search Institute, Summer 1997, 11.

"The Difference Regulation Makes." *Assets.* Search Institute, Spring 1997, 13.

"The 'One Thing' Teens Want?" in Snapstats, *Youthworker,* March/April 1998, 17.

"What Should Parents Monitor?" *Assets.* Search Institute, Autumn 1996, 12.

"Where Are Parenting Skills Learned?" *Youthworker,* May/June 1998, 18.

Benson, Peter. "Family Patterns Today." *Education Digest,* February 1995, 47-48.

Chapman, Gary. "Teen Love Language." *Living with Teenagers,* February 1998, 10-12.

Christie, Les. "Positive Discipline." *Living with Teenagers,* July 1998, 14-16.

Devries, Mike. "A Word to the Wise." *Living with Teenagers,* March 1998, 14-16.

Fernandez, Elizabeth. "Grim Legacy of Divorce." *The Atlanta Journal-Constitution,* June 3, 1997, F5.

Greene, Karen. "Parental Involvement with Teens." *Living with Teenagers,* September 1998, 22-23.

Justice, Mike. "Renegotiating the Rules." *Living with Teenagers,* September 1998, 14-16.

Kitch, Carolyn. "How to Talk So Your Teen-ager[sic] Will Listen." *Reader's Digest,* May 1997, 106-10.

Martin, Gail Gaymer. "Taking Off the Gloves." *Living with Teenagers,* March 1998, 10-12.

Minton, Lynn. Lynn Minton Reports: Fresh Voices, "Do Your Parents Ask You More Than You Want to Tell?" *Parade Magazine,* July 19, 1998, 12.

Lynn Minton Reports: Fresh Voices, "How Private is a Teen's Room?" *Parade Magazine,* July 21, 1996, 13.

Mueller, Walt. "Rediscovering Love." *Living with Teenagers,* February 1998, 9. "Virtual Parenting." *Living with Teenagers,* September 1998, 10.

Rodgers, Joann. "Notes under the Bedroom Door." *Psychology Today* 22, November 1988, 31-32.

Rosemond, John. "Quality of Child-rearing Provides no Guarantees." *The Atlanta – Journal Constitution,* July 17, 1998, C2.

Shapiro, Laura. "The Myth of Quality Time." *Newsweek,* May 12, 1997, 62-71.

Smalley, Gary, and Greg Smalley. "The Secret to Raising Teenagers: A Bountiful Bank Account!" *Living with Teenagers,* July 1998, 24-26.

Smalley, Greg, and Michael Smalley. "Got Conflict with Teens? Communicate!" *Living with Teenagers,* April 1997, 20-21.

Still-Pepper, Jim. "Just a Little Respect." *Living with Teenagers,* July 1998, 17. Internet

Gallup Youth Survey, *Emerging Trends,* September 1997. www.emergeonline.com/trends.

Gwynne, Robert. "Maslow's Hierarchy of Needs." funnelweb.utcc.utk.edu/ ~ gwynne/maslow.htm.

Maginnis, Robert L. "Family and Parenting Matter," a speech delivered at the San Diego County's third Substance Abuse Summit, December 12, 1997. www.frc.org/frc/podium/ pd98a 1 fs.html.

Pierce, LuAnn. "Dysfunctional Families: What Does That Mean?" www.wowwomen.com/tapestry/ arch_sane/dysfunctionalpt 1 .html.

Wendel, Peter. "Counseling Children of Divorce." *Counseling Today Online,* September 1997. www.counseling.org/ctonline/archives/CT0997/ct) 99 7al0.htm.

"Friends, Not Ads, Sway Teen Choice of Tobacco and Alcohol." www.eci-whoswho.com/highschool/ speakup/parents.html.

"Factors that Affect Children's Use of Drugs." Family Research Council: *In Focus,* 1998. www.frc.org/frc/ infocus/ef9864dr.html.

"Tuned-out Teens Are Bigger Threat Than Violence, Drugs, Limited Funds." www.eci-whoswho.com/ highschool/speakup/parents.html.

STEPFAMILY FOUNDATION, site updated April 17, 1998. www.stepfamily.org. "What Are the Stressors in My Life?" www.green-river.com/session2.html. "Who's Who Special Report: 'What Parents of Top Teens Don't Know About Their Kids Confirms Parents' Worst Fears." www.eci-whoswho. com/highschool/speakup/ parents.html.

Leaflets/Reports

U.S. Department of Education, National Center for Education Statistics. *Youth Indicators,* 1996. NCES 96-027, by Thomas Snyder and Linda Shafer. Washington, D.C.: 1996.

RESOURCES

FOR MORE RESOURCES TO HELP YOU WIN AT HOME AND LIFE CHECK OUT

THEWINNINGFAMILY.COM

www.ingramcontent.com/pod-product-compliance
Lightning Source LLC
Chambersburg PA
CBHW050855160426
43194CB00011B/2162